Psychotherapy
and the
Grieving Patient

Psychotherapy and the Grieving Patient

Edited by
E. Mark Stern

Psychotherapy and the Grieving Patient was originally published in 1985 by The Haworth Press, Inc. It has also been published as *The Psychotherapy Patient,* Volume 2, Number 1, Fall 1985, E. Mark Stern, Editor.

Harrington Park Press
New York • London

ISBN 0-918393-24-8

Published by

Harrington Park Press, Inc.
12 West 32 Street
New York, New York 10001

EUROSPAN/Harrington
3 Henrietta Street
London WC2E 8LU England

Harrington Park Press, Inc., is a subsidiary of The Haworth Press, Inc., 12 West 32 Street, New York, New York 10001.

Psychotherapy and the Grieving Patient was originally published in 1985 by The Haworth Press, Inc. It has also been published as *The Psychotherapy Patient*, Volume 2, Number 1, Fall 1985.

Library of Congress Cataloging in Publication Data
Main entry under title:

Psychotherapy and the grieving patient.

    "Originally published in 1985 by the Haworth Press, Inc. It was also published as the Psychotherapy patient, volume 2, number 1, fall 1985."
    Includes bibliographies.
    1. Loss (Psychology)—Addresses, essays, lectures. 2. Grief—Addresses, essays, lectures. 3. Psychotherapy—Addresses, essays, lectures. I. Stern, E. Mark, 1929- . [DNLM: 1. Death. 2. Grief. 3. Psychotherapy.
W1 PS87 v.2 no.1 / WM 420 P97535]
RC455.4.L67P79   1985b   155.9'37   85-17619
ISBN 0-918393-24-8

CONTENTS

Introduction

Grief is both destiny and possibility for all who care. Inherent in the sadness of loss is the potential for emotional gain and a renewed contract with life. As Thomas Mann has so eloquently stated, "To meet adverse conditions gracefully, is more than simply endurance; it is an act of aggression, a positive triumph." As an act of aggression, grief links itself to the larger picture of survival.

But despite heroics, personal loss is experienced on levels often linked to pernicious emotional pain. In cases of such agony, helplessness and rage may pose real threats to emotional health. Yet where throbbing agony fails to make an impact, a feeling of ennui may well dull the human condition. A true relationship to one's self can only exist beyond both the denial and the dread of loss.

Grief as a patient attribute enlists the psychotherapist's help in restoring and reestablishing a useful review of the memories of lost persons, places, and objects. Trained in the fine arts of listening, regrouping, and confronting, the psychotherapist endows grief with the appropriate task of enlarging life's repertoire. Without tragedy as a constituent element of this repertoire, personal experience would have little relationship to the legitimacy of history. Becoming fully responsible in such a sense allows grief to become its own legitimate remedy.

The contributors to this volume link arms in their respective presentations of grief and grieving as palpable attributes of awareness and vitality. The fallout from grief is awesome, spelling out the need to consciously leave behind that which was actually lost. Paradoxical as this may sound, it nevertheless stands as the rockbed of sanity.

Perhaps more than any other attribute of being alive, the psychotherapist is not exempt from the personal experience of grief. Some articles that might have been printed in these pages needed to be aborted because of a therapist's unreadiness to share what is still not digested. What does appear in these pages is a fine blending of the objective/subjective participation in the grieving process. Every effort has been made to create a sequential order of contents. Ultimately it will be up to the reader to participate in this dialogue on personal as well as on professional terms.

E. Mark Stern
Editor

Three Instances of the Emergence of Grief

E. Mark Stern

ABSTRACT. Two incidents, one dealing with denied but latent personal loss and the other with misappropriated grieving, are presented as illustrative of patient attributes. A third case, highlighting a patient's suicide, confronts the complexities of a therapist's involvement and grief.

SAD GRACES OF GOOD GRIEF

Good grief is the laughter of the angels. It is made in part of the snickering of having survived an enemy. More to the point, it is the exhilaration of what it means to survive a loved one. Total laughter is the expression of deepest living. With no object in mind except the staying power of mortal endurance, this ecstasy of laughter is the storage vault of memories. It is only the survivor who remembers. The survivor makes a fool of death.

*   *   *

Jenny was referred to my office on the heels of learning that her husband was gravely ill and would not be expected to live for more than a few months. He had lately suffered several significant heart attacks. Ted's chances for lasting through the year were meager.

Admittedly she had never set foot in Ireland, but somehow Jenny's words were punctuated by an occasional lilt, suggesting a natural Irish brogue. Later I was to discover that her mythical foundations served as her link to the romance of a distant land.

Jenny lived with the conviction that she was a reincarnated self. Her inner journeys appeared to bridge the wellsprings of mythical continents and lost eras. It seemed to me that these lapses into fantasy were her primary means of distancing herself from life's current realities. Yet there

E. Mark Stern, Ed.D., completed his clinical studies at Columbia University (1955) and at the Institute of the National Psychological Association for Psychoanalysis. Besides his private practice in psychotherapy and psychoanalysis, Dr. Stern is Professor in the Graduate Division of Pastoral Counseling, Iona College, New Rochelle, New York, and on the faculty of the American Institute for Psychotherapy and Psychoanalysis in New York City. Dr. Stern is a Diplomate in Clinical Psychology of the American Board of Professional Psychology, 215 East 11 Street, New York, NY 10003.

3

could be no escape without a hefty price. According to Bruno Bettelheim (1977), "those who live completely in their fantasies are beset by compulsive ruminations around some narrow stereotypical topics" (p. 119). Despite this obvious tendency to remain fixed in her ruminations, Jenny's fantasy visits to other times and places were, to her, part of an extended world view. Thus, from one point of view, these disassociated states were adaptive even as they channeled her withdrawal. To be precise, each time Jenny emerged from one of her fantasy episodes, she appeared somewhat better equipped to deal with day-to-day challenges. One such challenge was Jenny's partially submerged fear of the imminence of Ted's death. She was able to temper her fears with the expectation of the ethereal personalities who daily emerged from her fantasies.

Jenny came to me through a cousin who had, with Jenny's permission, called to tell me that the family considered Jenny to be bewitched. Several relatives apparently considered Jenny's brogue as evidence of her "possession." Through it all, Jenny considered her detached states to be a means of entering into communion with other selves.

In time, Ted died. He was 17 years older than Jenny. A simple Catholic wake was held. Those who came to greet Jenny with Mass cards and words of solace were, by her admission, put off by her exhilaration. "It's OK," she sprightly said to Clara, one of Ted's old friends who was deeply affected by his death. And to me she explained, "I felt I was bringing Clara a special greeting from all those who had departed." Jenny was aware that something in her behavior was almost too propulsive. Yet the almost manic momentum she experienced hardly permitted her a chance to regear the necessary day-to-day considerations.

In our early interviews I proposed the usual questions about what it was she felt she might be missing out on with Ted's departure from her life. Almost surreptitiously, I asked if there might not be something to be gained from Ted's death. Very little surfaced beyond some denial. Jenny had, from the earliest days of their marriage, denied Ted's place in her self-contained existence. "Intimate" relationships had already been established on a fantasy level. Through all I heard, I remained concerned that Jenny had not yet mourned the loss of Ted. Was she angry with him for dying? Or had she already done her mourning after any one or more of his several heart attacks? Frankly, I could determine no sign of overt anger at either the illness or the death. Either would have been a prelude to grieving.

Finally a memory emerged. As a 7-year-old child, Jenny had witnessed the death of her maternal grandmother. She had been alone in the family apartment at the time of her grandmother's fatal collapse. As the story emerged it became obvious that Jenny needed to develop "caretakers" (the fantasy personalities) of her own making who were meant to sustain her until her parents came home. Her childlike devotion to the image of

Mary, the Blessed Mother, served to enhance the work of these care-takers. Respectful of this devotion, I acknowledged how her grand-mother's death had allowed for an even deeper bond between Jenny and the universal Mother. Yet I wondered if there hadn't been times when Jenny feared the Virgin's absence. She cried. She so wanted her devotion to be have been blind and complete even in the face of the Virgin's failure to successfully intercede with God for her. Yet Jenny was both willing to be patient and willing to fill in for the lapses of the Blessed Mother. In response to my inquiry as to whether she felt any sorrow in the face of her heavenly Mother not always being there for her, Jenny's memories re-turned to the time of her grandmother's collapse. She recalled talking to the body, but, in her childhood wisdom, not waiting for an answer. In her own way, Jenny knew that the familiar love and comfort from her grand-mother would never again be part of her world. Rather than allowing the early imprint of this lack to interfere with her desire for solace from the caretakers, fantasy became her solace. It expressed itself as a conse-quence of the terror of not being responded to.

Given the depth of her aloneness, I could begin to understand her hesi-tation in giving her memories of Ted much of a chance. For Jenny, all that was left was her secret world of comforters. In a way I thought she'd understand, I mentioned this to her. "Are you suggesting a seance?" she quipped. I commented that some such sort of event had already been hap-pening within our encounters. She then asked me if I had been in touch with Ted's spirit.

"Try me," I replied.

Jenny (addressing Ted through me): "Why did you marry me if you knew you might soon be dead?"

EMS: "Who better to marry than the one I knew could best accept my dying?"

Jenny's eye caught mine. She was visibly angry. "Was that meant to be an insult?" she asked.

EMS: "You feel insulted? That's the real issue . . . . What answer would you have preferred?"

Our "seance" came to an abrupt ending. She appeared to pout. Even-tually her anger surfaced, allowing her to scold me for my lack of sen-sitivity.

EMS: "What would you rather I had said?"

Jenny: "The truth of the matter is that you made a lousy Ted." (With that she laughed and laughed and finally cried.)

EMS: "What would Ted have said to you?" (I persisted as I handed her a broken box of Kleenex. Her tears and her laughter were indistinguish-able.)

"It's OK," she murmured. It finally seemed all right to Jenny for him to have courted and married her.

Jenny: "Wouldn't you know that I would have fallen for a dead man?" Now she laughed as a prelude to her mourning. At first I wasn't sure how to respond. But soon I found myself laughing too. We had finally both tasted the good/sad graces of grief.

ANTICIPATORY LOSS

Of him I love day and night I dream'd he was dead,
And I dream'd I went where they had buried him
   I love, but he was not in that place,
And I dream'd I wander'd searching among burial places
   to find him,
And I found that every place was a burial place. —Walt Whitman

It was deep into the night when the phone rang. As I recall, Lyle had never phoned before except to occasionally rearrange an appointment.

"I feel harassed," he said. "I can't keep my father out of my mind. He keeps dying in my dreams, but all that's rational in me tells me that he's not dead."

Lyle, even at age 27 was a *puer aeternus,* an eternal youth. He'd failed all five courses in his last attempt as a student at a "second-rate" college. An internship program at a nonprofit arts foundation had provoked some interest in administrative work. And while he had his father to thank for "the connection" that landed him the internship, something inside kept telling him that, in the end, he'd never make it on his own. The realization of this career block caused him great consternation. A few days into the internship, Lyle felt a compelling impulse to tear at everything and anyone within reach. This destructiveness served to intensify Lyle's persistent anxiety. And the intensity expressed Lyle's terror of the unknown.

His fears accounted for his turning up a half hour late for his first appointment with me. What time remained was filled with grave concerns about his father. Lyle feared that his father might die before he had reason to be proud of him.

"What makes him hesitate in giving you his blessing?" I asked.

"How the hell am I supposed to know?" he replied. I had the feeling that what he said to me was more a "zinger" than an honest reply.

Lyle was consistently late, though he never failed to check in for the few remaining minutes of any given session.

"Why do you bother?" I once asked.

"I do try to get here and, even though I know you won't believe me, I invariably get waylaid." A multitude of distractions lay at the base of these delays. He preferred buses to the more rapid subway. But even more deterring was Lyle's penchant for window shopping. Yet for all the looking, he rarely made a purchase. Tentativeness was his bridge to life: choosing a "best time" to leave; whether he'd walk or take public transportation; or whether he should combine a visit with various errands filled Lyle's life with indecision. And just as plans always became thwarted, so too his angry impulses felt beyond his conscious control. "Someday," he warned, "I could do something I might regret."

"Like?"

"Oh, dump your ashtray on the floor."

"Or?"

"Or start to cry."

"And?"

"Never know the end of it."

So here we were. A young man, fearful of his every move—fearful of encounters; terrorized by decisions; and furthermore convinced that he was a grievous disappointment.

"But what else?"

"I fear that every day my father is dead."

"Wouldn't you know about it? Wouldn't anyone tell you? Your mother?"

"She's as bad as I am. Whenever he was late or angry or even coughed she was sure he was dead or on the verge of it."

"She any better these days?"

"If you call handing me the fears being better, then who knows?"

I imagined how it must have been for Lyle, day after day, fearing his father's death. It was obviously hell. But even the hell of one's sense of the inevitable needed to be warded off. So it was no surprise to discover that Lyle had his own bevy of prophylactic rituals.

"I may want to break things. If a person you love dies, you're supposed to cut your clothes."

Lyle recalled that, when he was a preschooler, his grandfather had died. And his father, fulfilling the classical Jewish tradition of mourning, cut a slit in his black tie. He further recalled his father explaining the tradition of "rending one's garments." Tearing things, and later breaking objects in advance of "the inevitable" became Lyle's gesture for warding off death.

"Do *you* feel broken?" I inquired.

"I *am* broken," he followed. "It's hell to be constantly living in anticipation of my father's death. And what's more, I can't see any relief on the horizon."

"What's it like when you invariably discover that he's alive?"

"I try not to get too worked up about it because I know that the fear could return in as little as 15 minutes." Even if his Dad took a brief walk "down the block for some cigars," he, Lyle, would "go bananas," dreading his father's final fate.

In effect, Lyle was trying to keep his father enshrined in a never-aging state. Perhaps he was less concerned about his father's welfare than he was of losing all remnants of his own youthfulness. By being hounded by his father's "death," he was in no qualitative position to enjoy his continuing presence. More than that, as long as his father was alive, Lyle could feel a reprieve from the inevitability of a life unencumbered by parental restraints. Yet the unyielding fear of his father's death continued to threaten his sanity.

Menacing fears of significant loss deplete positive narcissistic self-containment. Crucial loss can, in some cases, dismantle one's sense of security. To better approach these threats, I eventually shifted the focus to other "losses." For example, Lyle was fearful that I would be unwilling to welcome him back to therapy if he decided "to take a break." I gathered that he was struggling with the reality of my presence in his life. As he reclined on the couch during his sessions, Lyle conspicuously struggled to ward off any and all glances in my direction. It appeared that he needed to check to see if it was *really* me who was there. At one point he made several polite inquiries into the state of my health after his having seen me struggle with a lower-back spasm. I asked him if it would help to know that I was doing everything possible to take care of my health. In the spirit of the metaphor, I went the extra distance by promising him never to exceed 55 miles an hour in my car. I further asked if he preferred me to use airplanes only when absolutely necessary. I rushed to inform him that I'd given up cigarettes. And suggested that, if I died, he would have access to a series of taped conversations I made on managing life's stresses. If he so desired, I promised to delay my aging processes but only on the condition he promised *never* to change.

"You mean," he said, "that it's OK for me to leave therapy?"

I replied, "If you are willing to trust that I will always be here if ever you decide to return . . . . I want you to know that you'll never have to worry about losing me. After all, I'm not in the habit of dying."

"Ouch! I guess I get the message."

My tongue-in-cheek approach was meant to establish a paradigm of his unreal world (Nelson, 1968). After he indicated that he'd gotten "the message," I asked Lyle what it all really meant to him. Grudgingly he admitted to his having to learn to live without me, even as I continued on my own life's changes. He, of course, drew the obvious parallels to his fear of his father's death. It took time for Lyle to face up to the many resentments he had about his father's insensitive interference with his personal freedom. Part of Lyle obviously wanted "to kill his father off" as a way of making him less a morbid necessity in his life.

Lyle's life was entwined with his false mourning. Nevertheless, his grief was real and needed to be acknowledged. By my establishing the correct therapeutic paradigm, Lyle's dependency was addressed as the cause of his grieving.

Ultimately Lyle was willing to make an attempt at living his own existence.

SUICIDE AND A THERAPIST'S GRIEF

That which in the dark world is a pang, is in the light world a pleasing delight; and what in the dark is a stinging and enmity, is in the light an uplifting joy. And that which in the dark is a fear, terror and trembling, is in the light a shout of joy, a ringing forth and a singing.

The dark world is therefore the ground and origin of the light world. —Jacob Boehme (1575-1624)

* * *

The absurdity and pathos of the life of suicide stem from the despairer's will to achieve—through suicide—his status as a moral human being . . . . As despair deepens, what had meaning now seems meaningless; what seemed meaningless is fraught with meaning. —Leslie Farber (1976, p. 76, p. 68)

Erin was twice her recommended weight. Nevertheless she never missed a chance at boasting about how willing she was to eat herself to death. Her working days were set against a backdrop of prolonged family struggles and quarrels. Yet through all the strife, Erin decided to remain at home with her elderly parents. Headquartering herself with her octogenarian parents became her way of getting to know them in their final years. Recently their lives were being shaped by major illnesses. As with many elderly, each illness tendered its own dreads. Erin, the dutiful daughter, was rarely free from morbid foreboding. What scant relief she found was sealed into suicidal fantasies. Although Erin never specifically announced her plans to destroy herself, a unilateral pact was being covertly set into motion, expressed only in fragmented messages. There was, for example, the dream in which she and her parents were holed up in a coal-mine collapse. Another dream found her fearlessly waiting for a firing squad to be set into motion. At one point, Erin expressed historical interest in the unholy alliance between World War II kamikaze pilots and their loyalty to the honor of their parents. Erin proudly dubbed herself "nothing but a kamikaze high flier."

She had been faltering in her job. Inaccuracies in her administration of a family-founded travel agency were beginning to result in massive dollar losses. Fumbles and concocted excuses did not bode her well with her brother. As Erin's nominal boss, he had reached his limit with her and was beginning to reluctantly push for her removal from a position of fiscal responsibility. But since the final word belonged to their father, Erin's job remained intact. According to him, there would be no "insurrection or family disharmony" in his lifetime. On the surface Erin was but vaguely aware of the hefty emotional price she had indeed been paying for such paternal support. Through it all, Erin began to feel blamed by her brother for continually taking advantage of her parents' various disabilities.

Erin had lately been spending the better part of her evenings and weekends locked in her room. By her own admission, she used these hours to heap curses on her brother and parents. For all that, she was fearful that, once released from her self-imposed isolation, she might cause physical harm to all concerned. From her therapy she claimed to be aware of her surreptitious undermining of the family business.

Concurrent with the start of Erin's psychological treatment, her mother had been involved in one of many bouts with an upper-respiratory infection. Overburdened and frightened by the possibility of her mother's dying, Erin said that, if she continued to live her own life unchecked, she might in fact lose her mind completely. She openly acknowledged that she had been failing at the agency. What she did *not* say was that she had started to drink to excess. Later she owned up to the possibility of being an alcoholic and that only after she came to see me while intoxicated.

Erin's life was dependent on the world her parents built. At age 38, she was still wondering if she would be able to sustain herself after her parents' death. Given so little gratification, Erin was fearful of the implications of autonomy. There hadn't been a day of sunshine in her personal life for as long as she could remember. She regarded the fact of her obesity as a built-in guarantee that she would not have to endure a long life.

Erin had once done some unsuccessful apartment hunting. But much time had since passed. Yet, according to her own estimates, she had almost "made it," having at that time "met" her ideal apartment. Not having the courage to sign the lease had added yet another self-deriding defeat. The fateful implications of her refusal to clinch this and other opportunities left her feeling dismal and empty.

As Erin's mother made one of her slow recoveries, our work *seemed* to be gaining ground. Note, I was not at that time privy to her late-night bouts of drunkenness. Therapy was in fact in some sort of precarious balance. For all of that and despite the inner rancor, she appeared to be searching for tidbits of hope.

"The message I *want* is that I can give myself some light. I've got to know that I have the ability to find my own way."

"Erin," I asked, "which 'way' do you want to find?"

"I'd like to have the willingness to be able to follow up on the courage my parents had in living all their years."

I didn't fully understand. Hadn't she presented her mother as an emotional invalid and her father as a long-time depressive? I wasn't sure of what she meant by the courage of her parents. Later, and then only as Erin began to decompensate, I came to understand that she had traded in most of her survival tactics in hopes of being unconditionally loved as a little girl. Perhaps the terror of having to chart her own course was a primary step in the process of her emotional decompensation. Any struggle against total helplessness required her enhanced creativity in order that newer strengths or defenses could be established. Clearly Erin seemed to lose hold of the demands of her developmental tasks and realities.

Daily Erin experienced persistent forebodings of her parents' death. The anticipation of such a loss appeared to require no small degree of uncommon inventiveness if she was to survive emotionally. Survival was questionable since all favorable opportunities had essentially died for her. Her parents' half-alive presence became for Erin a murky sign of her lasting dependence on them.

Eventually Erin's father died. He flatly refused to be treated in the hospital after developing severe upper-respiratory symptoms. Erin responded to her father's illness by devoting herself to around-the-clock nursing. For the first time, she regarded herself as indispensable. As Erin rarely left her father's side, our sessions increasingly took place over the telephone. But while she found it necessary to miss several sessions, she always did so with the stipulation that I continue to reserve the time for her.

On a day she was least expected to appear in person, Erin came in seemingly bursting with joy. Soon after taking her place, she bowed her head while telling me that her father had died earlier that morning. About her? "Oh, don't worry," she said, "my heart is inclined to joy." According to Erin, her father "took sick" around 2 a.m. The doctor in their building who had been alerted to the possibility of an emergency had called an ambulance. All to no avail. He died on the way to the hospital.

As her story unfolded, my concern filled my eyes. "Oh, you mustn't," she said. "Wonders never cease. He's in heaven. I'm absolutely sure of that."

I asked about burial plans. Was there to be a wake? "No." But then again, "Yes," but only a brief gathering prior to the funeral Mass. Knowing her family to be steeped in Catholic cultural mores in which a traditional 2- or 3-day wake was the norm, I asked, "And how does the rest of the family feel about your plans?" As I suspected, Erin had not bothered to ask. I was later to learn that she had approached the funeral home some months earlier in order to pick out plain boxes for her father and mother. Later still I was to learn that not only had she taken it on herself to make pre-death arrangements for both her parents, but for herself as well.

The details of her father's funeral arrangements were quickly passed over. At the time, Erin's new level of excitement had obviously eclipsed her morbidities. On the wings of this elated state, Erin had made a decision to halt her excessive drinking and eating. Only then was I made aware of the amount of alcohol and junk food she had been consuming. As the weeks went on, Erin began to rapidly lose weight and was becoming better groomed. She began an almost manic uncloaking of positive plans for the future. Sad to say, there was a surprise that she had skillfully concealed.

Several months passed. Among her many "positive" plans, Erin had arranged for a family trip and reunion in Paris. She would be sending her mother, brother, sister-in-law, and their two young children on ahead. Her tack was to follow along a few days later, allowing time for her to complete some lingering work she had committed herself to do for the travel agency. In line with her glowing enthusiasm, the Parisian trip was to be part work and part pleasure.

As with the erstwhile funeral arrangements, Erin now took complete command of the family's Paris itinerary. The "power" inherent in her exhilaration remained uncontested by one and all. Though I had serious qualms about her new mood, her mask of deception withstood my several challenges. Despite my having made arrangements for medication, I could find no way of drawing in the reins on Erin's energetic manic abundance.

On the day Erin's family arrived in Paris, she called to tell me that she had just burned what remained of her father's private papers. She claimed she had destroyed "wads of paper" in the service of uncluttering her family's concerns. I was surprised and not a little shocked. The possible financial and legal implications following loss of essential documents could have been serious. I mentioned this to her with some concern in my voice but Erin concluded that she was justified in this take-charge behavior. Strengthened in her own defense, she contended that her father's last will and testament had been sufficient to give everyone the needed guidance required for the disposal of his remaining funds and property. As it turned out, Erin had indeed destroyed numerous financial instruments, many irreplaceable.

Erin's plans for going to Paris coincided with my first day of vacation. I was called to the phone minutes after my family and I arrived at our country house. "Just wanted to tell you," she said in an unmistakably intoxicated voice, "that I missed my flight."

I did my best to keep her on the phone.

Tragically, it was too late.

Attempts to get the police to enter her apartment met with little success. The weekend had come and the family travel agency would be closed through the following Tuesday. There was simply no way to reach Erin's family. I suspected the worst, even as I remained helpless to do anything.

Erin's brother called on Tuesday morning.

When Erin failed to show in Paris, her mother called and deputized the building superintendent to enter the apartment.

An empty pill container and a half-finished bottle of liquor were discovered next to Erin's body. Her brother told me she died in their late father's bed. She left no note.

My own shock and sense of helplessness soon gave way to grief. Significant traces of that grief continue to remain 12 years later. In the months following my vacation a studied awkwardness colored my approaches to patients. Partly I was concerned with my own role in Erin's suicidal pact with herself. These feelings eventually eased as I finally began to reconstruct Erin's therapy. In so doing, I became aware of how she did everything she could to shut me out along with the rest of the world. It was as if there could be no curative transformational process as long as her parents maintained the authority they did. For Erin, gaining her father's love and approval literally meant wedding him in eternity.

About a half year later, I made plans to give a workshop at the annual midwinter convention of the Division of Psychotherapy of the American Psychological Association on the effects on the psychotherapist of a patient's suicide. Having once decided to do the workshop, I became acutely aware of the need to confess. And so I confessed my concern about the possibility of an unconscious pact with Erin. At the same time, I began to understand the manipulativeness of her covert operations. Hadn't she been able to commandeer me, her therapist, into being one of her chief mourners? Who knows? Certainly Erin's lack of cooperation and honesty were meant to bring me into her self-destructive orbit. My answers to these concerns were foreign to the questions. Given a lack of cooperation and honesty, it is difficult to conceive of authentic recovery.

In a memoir published about a year after the suicide (Stern, 1973), I conceded that Erin, along with a close colleague and friend who had killed himself some years before, were now both historic components of my own sense of self. Such enigmas had become urgencies of my own grieving process.

Beyond several schooled guesses, I'll never know for sure the many sides of Erin's plot. And I doubt if I'll ever fully comprehend how I might have been an unwitting witness to these long-term plans. I've often said that, once a person establishes an internal suicide pact, all remaining problems appear manageable. If one knows the date of one's death, is there anything one cannot bear? More than likely, Erin's last years ushered her into an appointment with death. As a therapist, I continue to experience echos of a persisting question, "What might I have done to prevent this death?" The question persists regardless of the cause of death. The non-answers probably represent a bridge to one's ultimate helplessness. Yet there is still that other overriding sensation that wastes no time in experiencing a certain fury at another's voluntary desertion of life. For me, this puzzled fury essentially replaced an agitated anguish. As still more time has gone by, resignation has been transformed into the realization that I am not the master of another's fate.

My effectiveness as a therapist can only be apprehended while my patient is alive and willing to stay that way. If I, in my role as listener and counselor, can provide the groundwork for autonomy and life, so be it! On the other hand, if I am unknowingly drawn into a seditious pact, then my grief must be enlisted in the service of sharpening up future awarenesses of suicidal potentialities. The case of Erin remains open even as it is closed.

REFERENCES

Bettelheim, B. (1977). *The uses of enchantment.* New York: Knopf.

Farber, L.H. (1976). *Lying, despair, jealousy, envy, sex, suicide, drugs, and the good life.* New York: Bantam Books.

Nelson, M.C. (Ed.). (1968). *Roles and paradigms in psychotherapy.* New York: Grune and Stratton.

Stern, E.M. (1973). No turning back. *VOICES: The Art and Science of Psychotherapy,* 9(1), 10-12.

Psychotherapy and Grieving:
A Clinical Approach

Mary A. Jansen

ABSTRACT. This article discusses the general concept of mourning and grief, both normal and pathological, and attempts to facilitate appreciation of patient attributes in the grieving process from a clinical perspective. Issues related to the process of redirection of grief into more appropriate and productive cognitive and emotional states are discussed.

SIGNIFICANT LOSS

The process of grieving is one which is experienced by every one at some point in time. We all grieve for the loss of a loved one, either via death or via the loss of an aborted love relationship. We also grieve for other lost opportunities such as failing health, traumatic disabling conditions, and deteriorating physical and mental capacities. The grieving process is a normal one which has been explained in detail elsewhere (Bowlby, 1969; Freud, 1917/1957; Parkes, 1972), although sometimes grieving becomes a pathological process that is intensified to the point that the individual is overwhelmed, cannot function, and cannot progress through the state of grief to resolution of the loss. These various kinds of losses and the significance they may have for the patient are discussed in more detail below.

KINDS OF LOSSES AND WHAT THEY MEAN

Loss of a Spouse or Significant Other

The death of a spouse or a significant love relation produces sadness, depression, anxiety, emotional detachment, and frequently anger.

Mary A. Jansen, Ph.D., is Dean for Professional Affairs at the California School of Professional Psychology, 1350 M Street, Fresno, California 93721. In this capacity, Dr. Jansen serves as Director of Clinical Training and is responsible for all applied clinical training in the doctoral program in Clinical Psychology. She also serves as Director of the Psychological Services Center where she is clinically and administratively responsible for delivery of mental health services to patients in the Fresno and surrounding areas. Dr. Jansen earned the Ph.D. at Kent State University where she specialized in clinical and rehabilitation psychology.

15

Depression following the loss may be related to the patient's feelings of helplessness and impotence. These feelings arise from the patient's inability to prevent the loss from occurring and subsequently from the patient's inability to control these new feelings of sadness, depression, and grief. As the patient realizes this lack of control, reinforcement of the patient's fear of impotence and helplessness occurs and a circular effect becomes apparent—the less power the patient has to control the grief reaction and the more depressed the patient becomes, the lower the patient's self-confidence drops and the depression and grief reaction continue to escalate.

Although prior to the death of the loved one the patient may have experienced a positive relationship with the significant other, following the loss the patient may feel worthless, defective, angry, and self-blaming because of perceived inability to prevent the loss from occurring. This can lead to feelings of shame and dejection because the patient feels that all hope for future significant relationships have been lost. At the same time, the approval of the patient's self, which was mirrored by the presence and acceptance of the other, has been withdrawn and the belief that that approval would continue can no longer be sustained. Without approval from the lost love object, a worthless self-image may emerge with subsequent shame and feelings of low self-worth. These feelings frequently lead the patient to become withdrawn and to detach from other important relationships that may provide the support which is necessary for the patient to begin to see him or herself as a worthwhile human being with a positive contribution to make. The loss of a spouse or significant love relationship may be viewed in light of attachment theory which provides a way of viewing the striving of all human beings for strong affectional bonds with significant persons in their lives. Attachment behavior is apparent when a person strives for proximity to another individual who is preferred over all others, and who generally is viewed as stronger and/or wiser, and as necessary to the happiness and existence of the first person. Therefore, when we are confronted with the death of someone to whom we are attached, our very potential for existence and survival may feel threatened. Without the strength and comfort of the one to whom we are attached, who is seen as necessary for our survival and happiness, great anxiety may be produced because of the overwhelming sense of aloneness which is felt. This reaction is especially marked in individuals who have not formed appropriate and successful attachment bonds with parents during their developmental years. When autonomy in the developmental process has not been achieved, future relationships may be formed that satisfy the unresolved and potentially neurotic needs of the individual. When these attachments are broken the neurotic character of the attachment surfaces and the impact of the loss is especially grave. When this occurs, the patient's reaction to the loss will most likely be overwhelming and produce dysfunctional behavior. The therapist will note this as a pathological reaction within the grieving process and the attachment neurosis which is exposed can be dealt with clinically.

The affective states described above work in concert with cognitive processes that trigger and reinforce the affective state. Following the significant loss, an individual may doubt the apparent goodness of the self and may come to believe that the self is no longer worthy. This follows from the individual's previous conceptualization of the self as a competent person and leads to a new conceptualization of the self as incompetent based on the individual's perceived inability to prevent the loss of the significant relationship. At the same time, self-directed hostility results from the belief that the individual is no longer worthy of being cared for and is no longer competent and strong. Anger and hostility may also be directed at the lost loved one for leaving the individual. These cognitive manifestations of grief can readily be challenged for their basis in reality. The patient who clings to inappropriate cognitive processes can be taught to challenge them using cognitive behavioral techniques. These techniques allow the patient the opportunity to relearn ways of thinking so that affective states such as depression and anxiety, which previously were reinforced by self-statements about the patient's worthlessness and inability to get along without the lost other, can be redirected to more healthy and reality-based thoughts and conceptualizations.

Loss via an Aborted Love Relationship

The loss of a significant other via the unwanted ending of a love relationship produces grief and mourning for the individual who did not wish the relationship to end. The affective and cognitive manifestations of this grief are identical to those that are seen when the love relationship ends via death. The potential for pathological grieving, especially when the relationship is one in which a true attachment bond has been effected, is greater than when the relationship ends because of death. When a true attachment bond has been formed, the remaining individual will continue to deny that the relationship is over and will frequently misinterpret signs and signals from the lost love in order to support this denial process. As a result, the grieving individual will continually strive to reestablish the relationship with the lost love, to whom the patient is attached. Since the denial stage of the grieving process will frequently be lengthened because of the patient's refusal to accept that the relationship is over, the potential for self-destructive behaviors, which elicit angry antagonism from the departed lover, increases. The patient is also primed for even greater questions about his or her self-worth because the significant lover willfully and deliberately ended the relationship. Therefore, in addition to having to deal with all of the manifestations of grief and potentially pathological grief, the patient and therapist must work very hard to confront the patient's assertions that if he or she were really worthwhile and indeed lovable, the significant other would not have ended the relationship. The patient's fear that a meaningful love relationship will never be sustained because of the unworthiness of the patient, may in fact be the most difficult cognitive process to confront. The resultant loss of self-worth, depression, and anxiety will be most overwhelming in those patients whose early attachment bonds have not been properly formed and in whom development of satisfactory autonomy has not been achieved.

Loss of a Parent

Patients' reactions to the death of a parent post special problems because of the possibility for resurgence of repressed and unresolved feelings of ambivalence and neurotic attachment. Although many patients handle the death of a parent in a normal and appropriate fashion, some patients may experience this loss as much more significant than others. Recent research has shown that if the patient feels responsible for the death of the parent, grief symptoms will be less easily remediated. Also, when the deceased is the patient's mother, grief is resolved more slowly; and when a patient has not anticipated the death of a parent, levels of anxiety can be expected to remain high for a longer period of time. It has also been demonstrated that when patients attribute blame for the death to specified others, grief symptoms decline less over time. Further, the more negative life stress which a patient has encountered, the less the patient can be expected to reduce pathological symptoms of grief (Horowitz, Weiss, Kaltreider, et al., 1984). These researchers also noted that in their subject population, patients were more likely to report that the death was totally unexpected. It is difficult to say whether or not these individuals had in fact been informed of the impending death and were psychologically unable to anticipate the event and emotionally prepare for it, or whether they were negatively affected by the death because in fact it was a genuinely unexpected event. It is also possible that these individuals retrospectively experienced the parental death as unexpected because they were emotionally unable to integrate the news of the death into their psychic awareness.

Because of the myriad of emotions which patients experience following this loss, current relationships will be at special risk for added stress. Often the anger and rage a patient may have felt about the lost person, or about the patient's inability to prevent the loss, may be transferred onto another with whom the patient is engaged in a current relationship. This potential is greatest with the loss of a parent, which may evoke suppressed feelings of ambivalence and which may be transferred to a current partner. This disruption in current relationships allows an opportunity for the therapeutic working through of previous ambivalence and negative self-images that are now displaced onto a current relationship. Within this process a more integrated self may be realized with the resultant potential for a more stable, healthy relationship. If the ambivalence is not resolved and the grief reaction becomes sustained and pathological, the impact of future losses on the patient may be proportionately greater because of the cumulative effects of the unresolved ambivalence and grief.

Loss of Functioning

When an individual's physical or mental capacities deteriorate or when chronic illness or disability cause loss of functioning, the individual is faced with a series of gradual and often insidious losses which cause a prolonged grief reaction. Frequently these gradual losses are successive and therefore the grieving process is almost a continual one during the time that the illness or disability is in a deteriorating state. The wide range of potential losses which may be experienced by an individual with a chronic illness or disability is outlined by Lewis (1983) and includes loss of control over life, loss of privacy, loss of social and role status, loss of fantasies for the future, loss of daily routine and sleep, loss of sexual functioning, and so on. This experience of continual loss may produce continued grief and certainly extends the concept of what is the normal time for bereavement or grief. As the grieving process continues, it may be easy to categorize it as pathological bereavement or grief, when in reality it is a normal response to continued losses over a lengthy period of time. At the same time, the chronically ill must come to terms with death and perhaps with the integration of earlier losses culminating in death. This may indeed be the most difficult grieving process to work with because of this continued and long-term loss of functioning, and hope for recovery (Krupp, 1976). Following resolution of the grieving period, the individual must absorb the full impact of these losses. Because this is so traumatic and difficult, there may be an inclination to deny the illness or disability, and the patient must be helped to overcome this tendency toward denial. Before the patient can move toward full acceptance of the lost potential, the tendency to deny the full impact must be overcome. The balancing of acceptance of lost functioning and potential, with realistic hope for as full a life as possible, is very difficult. Continued support from loved ones who accept the patient in spite of declining potentials is necessary as is social contact with others who are facing similar situations. Although the continued progression of most illnesses and disabilities makes the clinical task a difficult one, acceptance of the decreased potential and opportunity give rise to increased possibilities for utilizing remaining capacities to the fullest extent. If the patient can be helped to view his or her remaining contributions as positive and necessary, acceptance and resolution will result in a favorable clinical outcome.

NORMAL VERSUS PATHOLOGICAL GRIEF

Whenever someone suffers a serious loss, either through death or through another unwanted separation, the individual experiences a range of psychological and physical states including sadness, a sense of dejection, loss of interest, anxiety, anger, questions about self-worth, altered states of appetite, sleep disturbance, agitated or depressed motor functioning, and withdrawal. When these expressions of grief become so inte _ified that the functional capacity of the individual is markedly reduced over an extended period of time, we generally assume that the grieving process is pathological rather than normal.

The key to identifying whether or not the grief and mourning associated with a significant loss are normal or pathological, is that in pathological grief the experience is overwhelming and intolerable. Each one of us who has experienced any significant loss has felt exceedingly sad, empty, and preoccupied with the loss and sense of aloneness. However, this normal mourning becomes pathological when the grief is overwhelming to the extent that the individual does not feel competent to handle the loss, but rather feels weak and abandoned, with a sense of dependency and fear of not being able to continue alone. It is the overwhelming and compelling quality of the sadness and fear which mark the grief as pathological.

It has been postulated that one major cause of pathological grief is the surfacing of self-images and role-relationship models which were present prior to the loss (Horowitz, Wilner, Marmar, & Krupnick, 1980). This theory postulates that an inadequate self-image and a model of inappropriate relationship roles were present prior to the loss but were suppressed successfully because of the presence of a positive relationship. With the loss of that relationship, the deficits in ego-esteem, self-image, and relationship of self to others become apparent to a pathological extent and the individual is overwhelmed. The clinical resolution of this pathological grief reaction lies in the therapist's ability to help the patient resolve the dependency issues which have surfaced, so that the patient's role and relationship to the lost person can be reevaluated. When viewed in light of attachment theory, it becomes apparent that resolution of the need for autonomy with the need for love and caring from helpful others leads to more appropriate evaluation of the patient's sense of self-worth and ego strengths. Once the patient begins to attribute positive outcomes to himself or herself, and comes to feel less dependent on external sources for sustenance of self-esteem, issues related to future attachments and fears of abandonment can be successfully addressed.

CLINICAL PERSPECTIVE: THE HIDDEN AGENDA

Patients who are grieving the loss of a significant relationship frequently present with complaints that may seem unrelated to the loss. An example of this is the case of an individual who initially presents a problem related to work and the potential loss of job title and resultant status. The problem is presented with stoicism and a sense of strength and intellectualization which can be seen as covering up for feelings which are too overwhelming to be addressed directly. Thus, these controlled affective responses may in fact be the result of the buildup of anger which serves as an armor to cover up deep sadness associated with the loss of this important relationship and subsequent damage to the individual's ego and sense of self-worth. A second purpose which the controlled affect serves is one of protecting the individual from further vulnerability from future losses of the same kind or of a different nature. We know that when an individual has not resolved a loss or has resolved a particular loss in an ambiguous way, future losses, which may on the surface appear to be completely distinct and unrelated, give rise to the unresolved feelings and trigger very deep emotional reactions. In order to protect oneself from these reactions, and to protect against this future vulnerability, the clinical presentation is frequently one of an intellectualized and controlled affective response. Clinicians who work with grieving patients who have intellectualized the affective response in this way are faced with a great deal of resistance. These patients invariably deny that there is any relationship between the presenting problem and a significant loss. In order to break through this resistance, the therapist must first assist the patient to achieve a willingness to let go of the intellectualized armor that protects the patient from vulnerability. If the patient can begin to consider letting go of this protective armor, then the therapy can proceed to the anger and deep sadness that exist within the patient. Breaking through the resistance is, of course, the most difficult task because frequently patients will say that they have dealt with the problem sufficiently and see no need to examine it further. Of potential benefit is the technique of asking the patient to externalize the presenting problem. Once the patient removes the visualized image of the "problem" from inside the self and makes it externally visible, the patient's entire persona changes. When this happens it is possible to see a distinction between the patient's state with the problem externalized and the patient's state when the problem has been reinternalized. The change is primarily one which is visible to the therapist because the patient becomes obviously vulnerable, more affective, and takes on a softer and more open appearance with the armor of the problem outside. Because of the dramatic nature of this work it is very difficult for patients in the initial stages of therapy to allow this to happen. Therefore, they tend to reinternalize the intellectualized problem despite verbalizations of wanting to be free, and they must continually fight to keep it externalized. This opens up an entire spectrum of possibilities for therapeutic work that are geared toward resolving the anger and prior sadness related to the grief and loss experienced.

It is only within the context of an exceedingly supportive psychotherapeutic environment that patients in this particular state can feel secure enough to even consider the possibility of allowing the intellectualized armor they have built up to be removed. Dealing with other forms of normal and pathological grief can be easier or more difficult depending upon the skill of the therapist and the resistance of the patient. As noted earlier, the degree to which grief is pathological is mediated by several variables including sex and relationship of the lost relationship, the preparedness of the patient for the loss, the social and psychological circumstances that the patient experienced at the time of the loss, and most important, the patient's premorbid personality. Depending on the formulation of attachment behavior and the integration of the patient's self, resolution of grief will be easy or difficult (Bowlby, 1980).

In order for therapy to be effective, the patient's energy must be refocused after resolution of the grief response. Patients must be helped to understand that grief and mourning are not only normal but are natural and that filling the void of the lost relationship does not mean that the patient cares less about the lost object or the relationship. It must be acknowledged that the lost relationship will never be replaced because the relationship that the patient had with the significant other is unique and cannot be replaced. However, other relationships which may succeed the lost one, although different, can also be of importance to the patient because they open the door for possible new experiences that the patient has not previously encountered. This in no way diminishes the patient's relationship with the lost significant other, but rather allows for the possibility of enhancement vis à vis a new relationship. If the patient's grief can be redirected in such a way that the patient can redirect energy from an intense search for the lost other, the patient can utilize this energy for more forward-looking, positive activities. Acceptance of grief as a natural process is therefore critical to the healing process. Likewise, the patient's acceptance of the concept of preserving the importance of the previous relationship while at the same time moving on to new relationships is also of critical importance. The ability to move on presupposes that the patient has resolved the anger, depression, and ambivalence that are the immediate and demonstrable products of the initial grieving process. Once accomplished, integration of the lost love and the potential for new and more appropriate interpersonal relationships leads to what may be seen as a positive consequence of the grieving process.

GRIEF WITHIN GRIEF—
A DEATH IN THE LIFE OF THE THERAPIST

When a death or major loss occurs in the life of a therapist, the potential exists for both positive and negative impact on the therapy process. Some considerations include the therapist's integration of this personal event and all of the issues which have been discussed related to the grief process including depression, hostility, and unresolved attributions which the therapist may have for the newly lost individual. Not only must the therapist in this situation work through these personal issues, but the therapist must also take care to ensure that these issues are not transferred to psychotherapy with current patients. Despite these cautions, a traumatic event such as this will impact on the therapy process. If the therapist is well integrated and capable of a healthy and appropriate grief reaction, the therapist can make an appropriate determination about how much of this personal grief can and should be shared with patients. If the therapist is not well integrated and the loss raises significant unresolved issues, the therapist may not be able to make appropriate and accurate decisions in this regard. Further, under these circumstances, the therapist may not be able to maintain enough objective distance to recognize when this personal event is interfering with the work to be done with patients.

In cases where the therapist can make the appropriate decision and decides to share this information with patients, issues such as the patient's ability to handle this kind of information must be dealt with. Patients may have a tendency to attempt to reverse roles with the therapist and begin to provide an excessive amount of support, ask probing questions, make interpretations about the therapist's reactions, and otherwise assume the role of the therapist. In these cases, patients may feel guilty about resuming their own therapeutic work at a time when the therapist is seemingly in need of assistance. Again, depending on the integration of the patient, the therapist's personal loss may be traumatic and this news may give rise to the vicarious experience of unresolved issues from the patient's life.

On the positive side, patients may be able to benefit from seeing the therapist as a more genuine human being who also experiences problems in living and in dealing with the loss of close relationships. Frequently this opens the possibility for increased growth because the patient is able to accept personal limitations that were previously unacceptable and is able to feel less threatened about genuine emotional reactions which have been experienced vis-à-vis traumatic events. The potential for role modeling in at least two realms is apparent. First, the patient may be able to recognize more appropriate ways of dealing with intrapsychic conflicts and may be able to discern that demonstration of the wide range of human emotions is not only acceptable but normal. Secondly, the patient may be able to learn more appropriate behavioral responses to situations such as the loss of significant others, and from this learning the patient may be able to handle situations more appropriately that in the past had been dealt with poorly. These new learnings and the behavioral success which follow serve to enhance the patient's sense of confidence and self-esteem and the therapeutic benefits can be greater than anticipated. However, because the potential for therapeutic gain or loss is great, therapists have a major responsibility to search their own awareness for answers to their competence to continue seeing patients following such an event, and form answers about their motivations for sharing the information with patients in the therapy setting.

SUMMARY

This article has presented an overview of the kinds of losses we experience that lead to the grieving process. When these losses resurrect unresolved issues that remain from earlier stages, such as failure to develop a sense of autonomy and resultant inability to form proper attachments, or when they resurrect unresolved feelings with current relationships, the grieving reaction and process will be pathological. Grieving will occur whenever a significant loss is experienced, including the loss of a loved one via death or via an aborted love relationship, loss of a parent, or loss of physical or mental capacity from advancing age or from chronic illness or disability.

When grieving is pathological its resolution is more difficult, and successful resolution depends on the patient's ability to review and revise misconceptions about his or her self-worth, ego-esteem, the nature of attachments, and the patient's ability to develop an appropriate sense of autonomy so that he or she can form loving yet independent relationships which allow for the continued growth of each other.

Of particular importance is the potential for the therapist's experiencing the loss of a significant relationship through death or an unwanted separation. When this happens, the therapist is faced with the prime responsibility for accurate introspection to accurately determine the appropriateness of continuing with therapeutic work, and the true motivational nature of the therapist's decision to inform patients of the therapist's personal loss.

This article has attempted to address the issues outlined above from a clinical perspective while at the same time focusing on the unique attributes which grieving patients bring to the therapy process. In so doing, a focus has been added on the ways that therapy might proceed to successfully redirect the patient's affect, energy, and thinking in more positive and integrated ways.

REFERENCES

Bowlby, J. (1969). *Attachment and loss,* London: Hogarth Press.
Bowlby, J. (1977). The making and breaking of affectional bonds. London: Hogarth Press.
Freud, S. (1957). Mourning and melancholia. In J. Strachey (Ed. and Trans.), *The standard edition of the complete psychological works of Sigmund Freud* (Vol. 14). London: Hogarth Press. (Original work published 1917).
Givelber, F., & Simon, B. (1981). A death in the life of a therapist and its impact on the therapy. *Psychiatry, 44,* 141-149.
Horowitz, M., Weiss, D., Kaltreider, N., Krupnick, J., Marmar, C., Wilner, N., & DeWitt, K. (1984). Reactions to the death of a parent. *The Journal of Nervous and Mental Disease, 172,* 383-392.
Horowitz, M., Wilner, N., Marmar, C., & Krupnick, J. (1980). Pathological grief and the activation of latent self-images. *The American Journal of Psychiatry, 137*(10), 1157-1162.
Kaltreider, N., Becker, T., & Horowitz, M. (1984). Relationship testing after the loss of a parent. *American Journal of Psychiatry, 141,* 243-246.
Krupp, N. (1976, Nov.). Adaptation to chronic illness. *Post-Graduate Medicine,* pp. 122-125.
Lewis, K. (1983). Grief in chronic illness and disability. *Journal of Rehabilitation, 49*(3), 8-11.
Parkes, C. (1972). *Bereavement.* New York: International Universities Press.

Grief and the Loss of Connection

Alexander Jasnow

ABSTRACT. Following Ernest Becker's hypothesis that the essential human need is to deny death, the author posits the corollary loss of connection not only with literal but with symbolic life continuity. Appropriate therapeutic attention, according to the author, converges with the strivings of religion and art.

Grief, in its widest and most universal sense, is the emotion we associate with the experience of loss. Perceived this way, grief takes its place in the pantheon of human feelings as one element in that affective spectrum that gives color to our existence.

These generalizations are meant to serve as an introduction to this essay, the purpose of which is to explore aspects of the emotion of grief from the viewpoint of a psychotherapist. I submit that they could serve equally well as the opening statements of a literary essay, say, on the tragic plays of Sophocles or Shakespeare. For that matter, they might also be appropriate as the beginning of a rather intellectualistic sermon on death and the consolations of religion. As psychotherapists, we deal necessarily with emotions, with states of feeling. It takes only a moment's reflection to realize that we are latecomers to a field that has been the center of human preoccupation since time immemorial. What is true of the emotions in general is true of the emotion of grief. Over the millennia there has been a vast outpouring of literature, both secular and religious in nature, dealing with grief and bereavement. This has long been the province of the poet and the priest. What do we as psychotherapists have to offer that is original and unique, different from that which has already been voiced by others? Folk wisdom has it, "Time heals grief." What have we to add to this succinct prescription?

Writing as a psychotherapist, I must acknowledge the fuzziness of the boundaries that separate us from the artist on one side and from the priest on the other. We have our own identity problem to content with. Are we compounding this problem as we intrude upon what is for us relatively new territory, that involving the grief-stricken and the bereaved?

It is true that we can refer back to the roots of psychotherapy in the ra-

Alexander Jasnow, Ph.D., is a psychotherapist in private practice in Fair Lawn, New Jersey. His mailing address is: 14-11 Lucena Drive, Fair Lawn, NJ 07410.

tionalistic ideology of the 19th century, and thus claim to be covered by the protective shield of Science. We can talk of objectivity of approach and methodological rigor as distinguishing us from the more subjective approaches of others. We do so at some risk, however, knowing the flimsiness and fragility of the evidence on which this claim must be based. In the scientific community at large, where distinctions are made between the hard and soft sciences, psychotherapy is generally perceived as a very soft science indeed.

All this, however, has become a moot point. In recent decades psychotherapists who for so long have concentrated on the problems of life are now turning with increasing intensity to the problems of loss and bereavement. The question of territorial rights becomes irrelevant in the face of this trend from a primary focus on Eros to increasing focus on Thanatos.

The use of the terms Eros and Thanatos is itself an implicit acknowledgment that the founder of psychoanalysis, Sigmund Freud, did not ignore the role of death in the development of the human psyche. It is, however, my impression that the concept of the death instinct has played an equivocal and secondary role in Freudian theoretical formulation. It is my further impression that, in general, theoreticians have focused on the earlier and middle stages of human development rather than on the psychological implications of impending death in oneself or others.

In this regard the names of Ernest Becker, Robert Jay Lifton and Elizabeth Kübler-Ross come most directly to mind. If such a shift in focus is indeed taking place, then the question that needs to be faced is "Why?"

One response is to cite the obvious. Psychotherapists do not live and work in a historical vacuum. All of us, therapists and patients alike, are vulnerable and reactive to the psychological climate unique to our times. Freud was to his and we are to ours.

If the origins of the psychotherapeutic movement are to be found deeply planted in the ideologies of the middle and late 19th century, then we must also recall that in retrospect, from the viewpoint of Western culture, these were halcyon days. Whatever the grimness of life for individuals and whatever the ominous prophesies of such Cassandras as Spengler and Nietzsche, for Western culture as a whole it was a time of expansiveness, optimism, and faith in the future.

The experiences of the 20th century have been traumatic. As a culture we have experienced a gradual erosion of optimism and of faith. We have undergone what might be called a loss of innocence. Like Adam and Eve, we have tasted the fruit of the Tree of Knowledge, our eyes are opening, and we have become aware of the presence of death in the world, death in a different guise than heretofore. High technology exacts a high price.

Since the opening years of this century, a period that also saw the beginning and massive development of the psychotherapeutic movement, a series of events of catastrophic proportion have taken place.

We have experienced a succession of disastrous wars, global in scope. These have been characterized by unprecedented slaughter, at times genocidal in intent and implacable in ferocity. With the last world war we have entered the nuclear age. For the first time in human history, the threat is not only to the survival of the individual but to the survival of the human species itself. Slowly but inexorably, this awareness is permeating our consciousness, changing our vision of human beings in the world.

I am aware that in one brief paragraph I have managed to cram in sufficient catastrophe to qualify as a doomsayer in good standing. There is a point to be made. If we observe our current historical situation with relative detachment, we cannot but become aware of the stresses which our society is experiencing. More relevant to the present issue is the effect that these stresses are having on the way in which we perceive death. We can postulate that each culture creates its own unique perceptual style, including the manner in which the phenomenon of death is perceived. Perceptual styles are subject to change in reaction to new conditions, new stresses. If this is so, then such shifts in attitude and perception may account, at least in part, for the intensified interest of psychotherapists in the phenomenon of death.

Ernest Becker (1973) has been a pioneer in this field. In his monumental work, *The Denial of Death,* he develops the concept that individuals need to build defenses against a direct awareness of death, if they are to lead a "normal" life. He postulates that there is an absolute need for the individual to deny his or her own mortality. There is a compelling striving to transcend the limitation on life continuity, set by the reality of our creatureliness. The direct, unmodulated awareness of mortality is assumed to be a source of overwhelming, paralyzing anxiety. Such panic states, destroying the capacity of the individual to perform life-maintaining functions, constitute a threat to survival. The repression and denial of such awareness enable the individual to function without the fear of massive disruption and paralysis potential in the situation. These then might be called the "normal" characterological defenses. They serve to maintain the essential illusion of personal immortality which makes normal life possible. It is this unusual vantage point that prompts Becker to title one of his chapter headings, "Human Character as a Vital Lie."

Becker outlines the interaction process between the culture and the individual. It is a process in which individuals create the culture, in part, out of their need for a vehicle for personal transcendence, for personal immortality. At the same time the culture serves as a means for transcendence, offering a range of modalities through which this can be achieved. Lifton (1979), who in his work critiques and modifies some of Becker's concepts, outlines five such modalities for achieving transcendental experience: the biological, theological, creative, natural, experiential. Since these can be utilized singly or in various combinations and permutations, a wealth of resources for transcendental experience exists—provided one has faith.

Buttressed with faith, the individual can approach death with equanimity, may even welcome it. One does so with the assurance that so doing, one steps through finite time into infinity. It was such assurance that comforted the Hindu widow performing the rite of suttee, that strengthened the Kamikaze pilot in his flight toward collision, that firmed up the will of the martyr dying for a cause. On a less dramatic level, it is the same faith and hope that gladdens the heart of grandparents seeing their grandchildren at play; that comforts us in seeing our names on buildings, on plaques at least, that promise to outlast us. However humble the means, there is the incessant search for that which will keep us connected with life in its continuity. Even as we grieve over the loss of a loved person or a valued object, so we grieve over the loss of a crucial connection with continuing life. And to lose faith is to lose the connection.

When a question of loss is to be faced, then we are back again dealing with the emotion of grief as reaction to loss. To experience a loss of faith is to experience a loss of connection. A loss of connection can impact on the individual with a wide range of affective intensity depending on the meaning of the loss. The emotional reaction may be one of mild irritation if what is experienced is a slight disruption in the flow of daily living. It can reach an extreme of despair if the loss is life-threatening or is perceived as such, since we are symbol making animals, life threats can be experienced on symbolic and mythic as well as on literal and concrete levels.

We may or may not accept Becker's hypothesis as to the nature of the "normal" character. Certainly it places the concept of normality within a different frame of reference from the one to which we are accustomed. It is a viewpoint that is closer to that of Jonathan Swift than it is to that of Sigmund Freud. Swift may still have something to tell us even in these times. We know that if defenses exist they develop from necessity. We also know that under given conditions of stress, defenses can decompensate. What can we anticipate if the hypothetical normal defenses against death awareness begin to decompensate under the pressure of massive chronic stress?

As psychotherapists, whatever our own defensive needs to deny and to repress awareness, there is that in us which seeks to uncover our deepest fears and apprehensions and to confront them as rationally as we can. This is our heritage. It is this striving, deflected and blunted as it must be by our need to protect ourselves from pain and terror, that must constitute a distinguishing aspect of our identity as psychotherapists. It is presumptuous to speak of fear, pain, and reason in the same sentence and with the same breath. Yet how else are we to explore the unknown where coping patterns of the past no longer fully suffice, where new coping patterns must be created?

It is rather strange to me, that writing as I do in the closing years of the 20th century, my associations go back to one other period of human history when the continuity of the human species appeared to be at risk. That was in the 13th century when the Black Death made its appearance and all human life was seen to be in jeopardy. Then the threat came from the outside; it was a force beyond human control. Today it comes through our own ingenuity. We carry death in our own hands. No wonder that that awareness of death is increasingly penetrating our consciousness and that our attention is increasingly focusing on problems of death and the threat to continuity. Is grief to become epidemic?

It is time to look more closely at the emotion of grief itself. The term "grief," like the term "love," does not fit easily into our therapeutic vocabulary. These words carry a heavy load of associational and literary baggage from the past. They are not scientific. Not so with the term "depression," which conveys a more objective, detached impression. The diagnostic manual published by the American Psychiatric Association (1980) lists a number of entries under the heading of "depression" but none at all under the heading of "grief." The closest reference to grief is the single entry, "uncomplicated bereavement" (code number V62.82). Does grief then constitute a psychiatric entity in its own right or is it another aspect of depression?

This is a question which practically answers itself. We can begin by making an obvious comparison:

> We have two individuals before us. One is designated as grieving, the other as depressed. Both are in an apparent state of despair. We note this by the expressions on their faces and the postures of their bodies. Both manifest psychomotor retardation, though there are also occasional periods of agitation. Both complain of a loss of appetite and of sleep disturbances. Both have difficulties in the area of attention and concentration.

Thus far, identical behavioral patterns have been described. The one clear difference between the two individuals is that in one instance these patterns followed upon a serious personal loss, the death of a spouse, while in the other no such specific event took place prior to the onset of the symptoms.

In short, we define grief as a depressive reaction to the experience of loss—what the diagnostic manual calls "uncomplicated bereavement." It becomes "abnormal" when the individual remains depressed and unable to function adequately after a "reasonable" period of time.

The experience of loss occurs within a social matrix, not in a vacuum—a matrix of interlocking relationships within a life-supporting environment. The impact and the meaning of the loss will vary depending on the nature of what is lost, but also on the particular stage of development of the individual involved and on the conditions existing in the environment. In an essential sense loss can be evaluated in terms of the extent to which it threatens the survival of the individual.

In the earliest stage of human development, in the embryonic neonate and infantile states, a loss of connection with supporting nurturant others obviously constitutes a direct literal threat to life itself. We know that early separation and loss of connection with essential others can leave scarrings and distortions in physiological and personality development. This we see in cases of infant marasmus or Spitz syndrome.

Whatever the difficulty, and perhaps impossibility, of trying to recapture the conscious experiences of infancy, those of us who have been lost as young children can perhaps recall the anguish of the grief that we felt. The intensity of parental feelings of loss are paralleled by the equal intensity of the child's feeling of panic.

Panic affects our experience of time. At the moment of panic, time appears to stand still. A gap appears in the very continuity of life itself. There is an unbearable yearning for reconnection and for a resumption of that blissful state in which continuity appeared to stretch out forever without threat of interruption. The future disappears and there is only the implacable present. The intensity of the feelings of grief and despair following severe loss accounts for the intensity of the feelings of relief and of joy when the lost is again found and life resumes its orderly path. Reconnection makes life continuity again possible.

I have spoken of being lost and being found. I might equally well be talking of death and resurrection.

In describing the impact of loss of connection at the earliest stage of human development, I have dwelt on the literal physicality of the threat to survival occasioned by such a separation. The abandoned infant cannot survive. The life-supporting elements must be reconnected or replaced.

The meaning of loss shifts through the various stages of human development even as the nature and quality of human connections change. Growth would appear to have aspects of accretion. Although loss of connection can always pose a degree of threat to the survival of the individual, the nature of the threat can incorporate symbolic as well as literal elements.

We come back again to the symbolism of death and resurrection—and we need to touch once more on the impelling human need to transcend finite creatureliness and to achieve and maintain, literally and symbolically, the essential connection with continuity of life. It is my thesis that the loss of the symbolic connection can itself be a cause for grief and despair, equivalent to the loss of a literal connection with the life-supporting system.

The achievement of the transcendent experience does not result simply from an act of will. It depends upon a faith system, one that is integral to a specific culture and that the individual has incorporated. It is through this process that the individual feels able to connect with a supportive system outside of self which holds out the hope of a continuity with the ongoing life stream—a promise of immortality. The loss of this connection through the loss of faith is a threat to the symbolic survival of the individual. That is indeed to become prey to despair and depression, to become aware of the presence of death in the most irreconcilable and implacable form.

At all costs we must maintain our connections with the continuity of life. But how do we do so at a time in our history when faith in all its manifestations has been so severely eroded? We are aware of the destructive effect on culture and on the individual within those cultures when their roots have been cut and faith systems shattered. There is little question that we are facing a survival crisis as individuals and as a culture. How do we maintain our faith when there is a threat, integral to the culture, directed at the survival of the human species?

If we keep in mind Becker's hypothesis regarding the essential human need to deny death, we may extrapolate on his hypothesis by considering what may take place if these defenses begin to decompensate. We might anticipate massive feelings of loss of connection not only with literal but with symbolic life continuity. Such feelings of loss would be accompanied by intense despair and depression. Life would lose its meaning.

I do not see psychotherapists as being in a position to provide answers to these feelings of basic loss. We, too, would be among the grief-stricken and the despairing. But I do not see that as psychotherapists we have the responsibility to provide the answers. We do have the responsibility to ask the right questions, to make the correct diagnosis. And since our basic commitment is to the survival of our patients, literal as well as symbolic, it seems clear that our basic need is to promote the survival of our species. Toward this awesomely simple goal, the strivings of religion, art, and psychotherapy have to converge.

REFERENCES

American Psychiatric Association. (1980). *Diagnostic and statistical manual of mental disorders* (3rd ed.). Washington, DC: Author.

Becker, E. (1973). *The denial of death.* New York: The Free Press.

Kübler-Ross, E. (1969). *On death and dying.* New York: Macmillan.

Lifton, R. J. (1979). *The broken connection.* New York: Simon & Schuster.

Imagery and Grief Work

Mary S. Cerney

ABSTRACT. After briefly reviewing the literature on imagery, the author presents a case study in which a young woman using imagery works through her unresolved feelings surrounding the tragic death of her father and younger sister. Hypotheses are then presented suggesting that imagery is effective because the subconscious mind cannot detect the difference between what is real and unreal. The author cautions that the use of imagery, however effective, may not be right for everyone or in all situations.

INTRODUCTION

I have discovered that unresolved grief prevents many patients from moving forward in their lives. This hypothesis evolved as I asked patients under hypnosis to go back to the origin of their difficulty. Time after time their thoughts centered on some loss that had not been adequately mourned. This loss could be a hope, a dream of what never was and never could be, a significant relationship, or the death of a loved one.

As my interest in loss and the management of grief evolved and became known, individuals asked for help with their grieving. Since my hypnosis patients had already taught me the effectiveness of using imagery in mastering difficult situations, it was a natural step to use imagery with patients who were struggling to cope with the loss of a loved one. Initially, I used hypnotic techniques to induce trance. But one patient was fearful of hypnosis so I asked her if she would mind imaging her husband. She responded that she frequently visualized him, so imaging should be easy. This patient and others also taught me that I did not need to induce trance because they spontaneously went into a light hypnotic trance when I asked them to image their loved one.

I have used imagery most frequently in dealing with what is usually termed atypical or pathological mourning, that is, mourning that has gone on too long and is interfering with the individual's life. In more recent times, I have found imagery can be used earlier to facilitate the normal grieving process.

In this article, I will briefly review literature relevant to my use of imagery, present a case study using imagery in grief resolution, and con-

Mary S. Cerney, Ph.D., is affiliated with The Menninger Foundation, Topeka, KS 66601.

clude with hypotheses on what happens in the course of the imagery work.

REVIEW OF LITERATURE

The research literature around imagery has exploded in recent years. An extensive review would not only be impossible but also inappropriate within the context of this article. I will, however, briefly look at the imagery work of some outstanding psychoanalysts whose work is more compatible with my theoretical framework.[1]

The use of imagery is not new even among clinicians who adhere to the psychoanalytic tradition. No one seriously interested in studying this approach to imagery should overlook the work of Joseph Reyher and Joseph Shorr. Reyher (1977) in his work has continued the classical free-association method emphasizing images rather than words. Shorr (1972, 1978) on the other hand, uses what he calls "psycho-imagination," a much more active intervention and direction, which employs numerous imaginative situations within the psychotherapeutic situation. My work has characteristics similar to both of these methods.

Although no specific method of imagery is credited to Horowitz (1968, 1970, 1978), another psychoanalytically oriented clinician, he has extensively investigated the role of imagery within cognitive psychology. Numerous insights invaluable to image therapists can also be found in the works of the neo-Freudians Harry Stack Sullivan (1956) and Eric Fromm (1951) and their followers, Tauber and Green (1959).

The case of Susan[2] who was struggling to cope with the tragic accidental deaths of her father and younger sister illustrates my use of imagery in grief work.

THE CASE OF SUSAN

Although Susan's father had been an alcoholic for many years, he did not join Alcoholics Anonymous until Susan was 10 years old. Even though he quit drinking, he continued to be physically abusive to his wife and children. They were all frightened of him and reportedly had never felt close to him. When Susan was 12, her parents divorced. Two years

---

[1]Readers wishing a more comprehensive review of the imagery literature should see *Imagery: Current Theory, Research, and Application,* edited by Anees A. Sheikh (1983); *Image Formation and Psychotherapy,* by Mardi Jon Horowitz (1983); and *The Power of Human Imagination,* edited by Jerome L. Singer and Kenneth S. Pope (1978).

[2]All names and identifying data have been changed.

later, her mother married Fred, a man who related well to the three children, becoming the father they never had.

For a time, all went well. Then the oldest child, Paul, age 20, began to argue with his mother and left home. Janet, Susan's younger sister, became rebellious toward her mother and left home to live with her natural father. After 6 months, Janet reconciled with her mother and wanted to live with her again. When the father and Janet were driving back to her mother's home their car was struck by a drunk driver and both were killed instantly. Janet was so severely mutilated in the accident, her casket could not be opened; the father too was badly scarred. Although the father's arm had been severed, this fact was concealed in the casket and was discovered by Susan later when she overheard some of her friends discussing the accident.

For over 2 years after the accident, Susan, now almost 18, continued to have nightmares while becoming more and more isolated and withdrawn from her friends. Her mother, aware of Susan's pain, offered her the opportunity to meet with me; Susan immediately called for an appointment.

Susan was an attractive young woman. Upon entering my office, she began to speak immediately of her difficulties since the accidental deaths of her sister and father. School had become increasingly difficult as she spent her time worrying about what might happen to her mother. Since she was a high-school senior, Susan said she should begin thinking of leaving home but she was afraid to do so. Her mother might feel abandoned and all alone.

Ever since the accident, Susan said she had had nightmares in which her father came to her wanting to talk. His wanting to talk puzzled her since he had never had time for any of his children when he was alive. Although in her nightmare she and her father seemed to talk the entire night, she could not remember in the morning what they had talked about. What she did know was that she would awake frightened and in a cold sweat. In the nightmare, she said her father was scarred, missing an arm, and looked like he did in the casket. "I have never seen anything look so dead," she shuddered.

I asked Susan if she would try to have the dream again of her father coming to her. She readily closed her eyes and said she could see him walking toward her. His face was badly scarred, he had no shoes on, and his arm was missing. I asked her if she would like to heal him. She brightened, agreeing immediately, "Oh, yes!" I suggested she take her hand and heal his face. Her hand went up as though she were touching his face. "His face is healed and there are no more scars," she announced, "but what should I do about the missing arm?" I told her it was lying next to her chair. She could pick it up and put it where it belonged. At first Susan said she could not see the arm, but I suggested she look again. "Oh, I see it!" she exclaimed and bent down to pick it up, placing it at her father's shoulder. Susan reported that her father was smiling now, but he still did not have any shoes. I suggested there was a pair on the other side of her chair which she could give him. Since he now had both of his arms, he could put his shoes on himself. With no hesitation, she picked up the shoes and gave them to her father.

I asked Susan what she would like to say to her father. First she wanted to know if she could see Janet. He told her Janet could not come yet. Susan then wanted to know why he acted the way he did when he was alive. I instructed Susan not to put words in his mouth, but just to listen to what spontaneously came to mind. Her father told her that he knew no other way. He had grown up in a home that did not know how to express love and he was sorry for how he had treated all of them.

Susan and her father carried on a lengthy conversation during which she acknowledged the irritations, the anger, and finally the caring that she had for him. They talked together until Susan had nothing more that she wanted to ask of him or say to him.

I asked Susan about her feelings for her stepfather as compared to her natural father. She said that when her father appeared in her dreams, her stepfather left. I suggested that she talk to her father about the stepfather. Her father assured her he approved of her relationship with the stepfather and was happy that she was now receiving the kind of fathering that she had always wanted from him.

Susan then reported that her father smiled, walked over to her, gave her a hug, and then turned to leave, waving good-bye. She could let him go because now she knew he was happy, and she was happy and at peace with him.

Within a few minutes Susan exclaimed, "I see Janet coming." Not seeing Janet in the casket had made it hard to accept her death. At the sight of Janet, Susan began to cry saying she didn't want to look and she was afraid. Janet's face and entire body were so badly injured. I asked Susan if she knew what could give her the courage to look at her sister. She replied, "No." I then inquired, "Would it help if I held your hand?" She uttered a relieved "Yes," and immediately extended her hand which I then held. I suggested that her love could heal Janet just as it had healed her father. Without hesitation, Susan raised her other hand sweeping over her sister's body healing it. She then smiled and relaxed, "Janet is completely healed and she is smiling."

I asked Susan what she wanted to say to Janet. She said that she wished she were in the car rather than Janet. Susan and Janet then talked about the jealousy feelings most older sisters harbor toward younger sisters. But those angry and guilty feelings were only a part of her total feelings and she spoke of her deep love for Janet and of the fun times they used to have together. They had become such good friends that last year, and Susan would miss Janet very much. Janet replied that it was important for Susan to be alive and not to worry about her as she was happy now. When the two of them had said all they needed to say to each other, Susan reported that she saw Janet carrying flowers and dancing away waving good-bye to her.

Susan was silent for some time. After a while, I asked her what was happening. She reported a happy memory in which her entire family was having a wonderful time camping. She had forgotten about that time, but she could clearly see her father, her mother, her brother, her sister, and herself enjoying the time together. I did not interrupt this memory until I saw her noticeably relax. I then suggested that when she was ready, she could bring herself back to the present.

After some time, Susan opened her eyes and began to talk about the difficulties of leaving home, the issue she could not work on while she struggled with the mourning process. Leaving home was perilous: Susan's brother had left home after an argument; Janet had left home after an argument. When Janet reconciled with her mother and was in the process of returning home, she was killed. Could Susan risk leaving home, or leave home in a different way, and what would happen to her if she did leave home? We spent the remainder of that session and another session discussing the implications of leaving home. A third session included mother and Susan. Mother assured Susan that it was all right to leave home, not only so Susan could get on with her own life, but also so mother could get on with her own life.

Susan required no further treatment. She moved out of her mother's home within the following year. At the time of this writing, over two years have elapsed since I met with Susan. She is currently living in her own apartment with a roommate, is dating, working part-time, and attending college.

DISCUSSION

This young woman readily used imagery to help her work with some unresolved issues surrounding the death of her father and her sister. Continuing to be absorbed in these issues prevented her from dealing with the age-appropriate fears and concerns surrounding her moving out of the family home and facing life on her own. Imagery gave her the opportunity to say to her father what she had not dared to utter when he was alive, to ask the questions she had been unable to ask, and to respond in a way she could not during his lifetime. With her sister, she could discuss some of her earlier unpleasant feelings, and she could share how much she loved her and how much she missed her. Perhaps imagery's main contribution in grief work is that it allows the individual an opportunity to handle unfinished business with the deceased. Feelings not expressed before can now be expressed, misunderstandings can be clarified, and memories can be healed.

Whether or not to induce trance when using imagery is a question each therapist may have to decide. When I asked Susan to have her dream of her father, she easily went into a light trance without induction. The research literature is of two minds on this topic: one, that induced trance will heighten the imagery experience (Orne, 1959); and the other, that it doesn't make any significant difference (Barber, 1965, 1969, 1971). I induce trance only when it is necessary to relax the patient who wants to image and is too anxious to do so.

The length of time required to work through unresolved issues will vary with different individuals. Susan spent less than half an hour actively using imagery. The process, however, does not go so quickly for everyone. Sometimes, an individual may require a number of sessions to work toward a resolution. Others may never let go of the deceased.

To use imagery appropriately, one must understand the meaning unresolved mourning has for a particular individual. Some patients cannot let go because the deceased has become an integral part of their sense of self. For them to let go would mean a loss of identity, a disintegration of the self, hence their struggle to hold on. The therapist can help the individual who cannot let go, by changing an evil or tormenting persecutor into a kind and benevolent helper who facilitates the patient's forward movement in life, somewhat like a guardian angel or internal guru.

On some occasions, when I think the patient has worked through all the necessary issues but the deceased individual still has not left, I may say to the patient: "What would permit you to let N.N. go?" The response the patient makes will guide the direction the imagery is to take. Frequently, the deceased individual may be ready to go, but the patient is not ready to let the individual go. That information suggests a number of possible solutions: There are still other issues to work on; there is a narcissistic core within the patient that must first be analyzed; and/or it may be important for the deceased individual to be integrated into the patient's life rather than helped to leave. It is not wise to force the patient to let someone go. For some patients forcing them can be extremely upsetting. Generally, a patient who does not want to let someone go will not let the individual go, regardless of what the therapist does.

It has been my experience that when the patient is ready to say goodbye, that is, to complete this stage of the mourning process, the individual being mourned will spontaneously leave as was seen in the vignette. Susan, without any prompting on my part, reported that her father was leaving. This departure is the treater's clue that the patient has completed the work that needed to be done at this time. Usually if this stage of the mourning process is complete, the individual will spontaneously report, very soon after the person has left, a pleasant memory involving the one being mourned. Susan reported a memory of a happy time when the entire family had gone camping. Prior to the imagery session, Susan had told me she had no happy memories of her father.

After sessions such as the one reported, some patients have mentioned that although they experience a sense of lightness and freedom, they are very tired as though they have let go of a very heavy burden. The best results from such work seem to occur when the patient takes time to rest or sleep after such a session. Some patients report sleeping soundly from 2 to 4 hours after such a session. It seems that in resting afterwards there is some integration of the work that has previously occurred.

Although imagery was most helpful for Susan, the use of imagery may not be helpful to or appropriate for everyone and in every situation. If the patient does not wish to use imagery, the therapist is not wise to use it. If the patient does not wish to continue an imagery session, the therapist can interrupt such a session by saying something like: "That is all right. You do not need to continue. When you feel ready, bring yourself back to the present." When it is evident that the patient is fully conscious, discuss the experience. Let the patient know that it is all right to stop. He or she is the best judge regarding if and when the use of imagery is appropriate.

Although a great deal of the research literature on imagery is somewhat confusing and contradictory, researchers who have examined the role of voluntary thought imagery in relation to affective processes agree on one point: It is effective and its effectiveness is well documented. Depending upon how well an individual can construct vivid imagery and become absorbed into its content, the consequences are remarkably similar to those that result from the actual stimulus situation. Although this belief has existed from antiquity (McMahon, 1976), only recently have researchers demonstrated it experimentally. Klinger (1980) states, "Experiencing something in imagery can be considered to be in many essential ways psychologically equivalent to experiencing the thing in actuality" (p. 5). He is not alone in this view (Kosslyn, 1980; Neisser, 1976; Sheikh & Shaffer, 1979). According to some studies (Perky, 1910; Leuba, 1940; John, 1967; Segal & Fusella, 1970) imagery and perception are experientially and neurophysiologically comparable processes and it is intrinsically difficult to distinguish between them.

Sheikh (1983), in summarizing what he and other researchers have concluded regarding why imagery is so effective, states that the "numerous mechanisms that presumably underlie the effectiveness of imagery in the clinic . . . almost equal the number of methods available" (p. 423). Meichenbaum (1978) suggests that three psychological processes explain the effectiveness of all imagery-based therapies. These processes are summarized by Sheikh (1983) as:

(1) the feeling of control which the patient gains as a result of ob-

serving and rehearsing various images; (2) the modified meaning or changed internal dialogue that precedes, attends, and succeeds examples of maladaptive behavior; and (3) the mental rehearsal of alternative responses that lead to the enhancement of coping skills. (p. 423)

Imagery generally occurs in a light trance which places one in touch with one's subconscious. Within the subconscious one experiences no difference between what is real and what is not real. Thinking at this level of trance in the concrete mode is similar to how we think during our developmental phase until about the age of 9, 10, or 11, and really never quite lose. In this mode we are all powerful, the center of all, and the locus of all control. We can do all kinds of things, such as heal a scarred face, replace a missing limb, and alter the world to our satisfaction. Our conscious mind, however, is not asleep. We are well aware of what we are doing. Although our conscious mind knows that our creation is a product of our imagination, our subconscious mind doesn't particularly care. The literature reports and I agree that dramatic results can result through the use of imagery when the therapist sensitively follows the patient's cues in facilitating the process.

In summary, although the literature cites dramatic results that can accrue from the skilled use of imagery, more controlled experimental research within the clinical area is needed. I concur with Sheikh (1983) who writes:

Overly enthusiastic image therapists perhaps should keep in mind that there was a time in history when the clinical significance of imagery was widely accepted, but that this period regrettably did not last. It is imperative that the creative surge be accompanied by sobering scrutiny, lest the future of imagery in the clinic be written in the past. (p. 424)

REFERENCES

Barber, T.X. (1969). A scientific approach to hypnosis. Princeton: Van Nostrand.

Barber, T.X. (1971). Imagery and "hallucinations": Effects of LSD contrasted with effects of "hypnotic" suggestions. In Imagery: Current cognitive approaches (pp. 102-130). New York: Academic Press.

Barber, T.X., & Calberley, D.S. (1965). Hypnotizeability, suggestibility, and personality. II. An assessment of previous imaginative-fantasy experiences by the As, Barber-Glass, and Shore questionnaires. Journal of Clinical Psychology, 21, 57.

Fromm, E. (1951). The forgotten language. New York: Rinehart.

Horowitz, M.J. (1968). Visual thought images in psychotherapy. American Journal of Psychotherapy, 22, 55-75.

Horowitz, M.J. (1970). Image formation and cognition. New York: Appleton.

Horowitz, M.J. (1978). Controls of visual imagery and therapeutic intervention. In J.L. Singer, & K.S. Pope (Eds.), The power of human imagination. New York: Plenum.

Horowitz, M.J. (1983). *Image formation and psychotherapy.* New York: Jason Aronson.

John, E.R. (1967). *Mechanisms of memory.* New York: Academic Press.

Klinger, E. (1980). Therapy and the flow of thought. In J.E. Shorr, G.E. Sobel, P. Robin, & J.A. Connella (Eds.), *Imagery: Its many dimensions and applications.* New York: Plenum.

Kosslyn, S. (1980). *Image and mind.* Cambridge, MA: Harvard University Press.

Leuba, C. (1940). Images as conditioned sensations. *Journal of Experimental Psychology, 26,* 345-351.

McMahon, C.E. (1976). The role of imagination in the disease process: Pre-Cartesian history. *Psychological Medicine, 6,* 179-184.

Meichenbaum, D. (1978). Why does using imagery in psychotherapy lead to change? In J.L. Singer & K.S. Pope (Eds.), *The power of the human imagination.* New York: Plenum.

Neisser, U. (1976). *Cognition and reality.* San Francisco: Freeman.

Orne, M.T. (1959). The nature of hypnosis: Artifact or essence? *Journal of Abnormal Social Psychology, 58,* 277.

Perky, C.W. (1910). An experimental study of imagination. *American Journal of Psychology, 21,* 422-452.

Reyher, J. (1977). Spontaneous visual imagery: Implications for psychoanalysis, psychopathology, and psychotherapy. *Journal of Mental Imagery, 2,* 253-274.

Segal, S.J., & Fusella, Y. (1970). Influence of imagined pictures and sounds on detection of visual and auditory signals. *Journal of Experimental Psychology, 83,* 458-464.

Sheikh, A.A. (Ed.). (1983). *Imagery: Current theory, research, and application.* New York: John Wiley & Sons.

Sheikh, A.A., & Shaffer, J.T. (Eds.). (1979). *The potential of fantasy and imagination.* New York: Brandon House.

Shorr, J.E. (1972). *Psycho-imagination therapy: The integration of phenomenology and imagination.* New York: Intercontinental Medical Book Corp.

Shorr, J.E. (1978). Clinical use of categories of therapeutic imagery. In J.L. Singer & K.S. Pope (Eds.), *The power of human imagination.* New York: Plenum.

Singer, J.L., & Pope, K.S. (Eds.). (1978). *The power of human imagination.* New York: Plenum Press.

Sullivan, H.S. (1956). *Clinical studies in psychiatry.* New York: Norton.

Tauber, E.S., & Green, M.G. (1959). *Prelogical experience.* New York: Basic Books.

Electra in Mourning:
Grief Work and the Adult Incest Survivor

Kate F. Hays

ABSTRACT. The adult incest survivor's experience is explored, using a paradigm of the grieving process. Stages of mourning are reviewed from the perspective of the child incest-victim's experience and the adult incest-survivor's personality and defenses. Therapy clients describe their own past and present experiencing of "closing off" (denial, confusion, numbness) and "opening up" to affects. Because of the multiple layers and levels of mourning, working through is a complicated process. The effects of this early and ongoing trauma seem lifelong. Even in resolution, scars are apparent.

INTRODUCTION

I've just become aware that there are a whole lot of issues I haven't even begun to deal with. They seem to pop out like cotton balls that I've stuffed into a tiny jar. It kind of startles me when they show up. I don't know what will come out. I don't know when it will come out. Wedged so tightly in that jar, I didn't even know there were so many. And I only wanted one cotton ball at a time. I don't know if I want to know about all that yet.

The image of a jar full of cotton balls of knowledge about incest and its effects is perhaps an apt metaphor for us all. Increasingly, attention to the subject is being drawn by the media. There has been an upsurge of profes-

---

Kate F. Hays, Ph.D., is a clinical psychologist and director of Twin Rivers Counseling Center in Franklin, NH 03235. A native New Yorker, she came to New Hampshire via the University of New Hampshire as an undergraduate, with a detour to Boston University for her master's and doctoral degrees. She has been in clinical practice for the past 14 years. She began leading a group for adult survivors of incest in May, 1984.

For sharing his thematic development of ideas pertaining to incest and mourning, the author would like to thank Albert Pesso. The support and suggestions of Kathryn Mehl, Leo Shea, Virginia Slayton, Terry Sturke, and Kathleen Sullivan are greatly appreciated. The women whose voices are quoted here articulate in anonymity the feelings of many.

45

sional inquiry and treatment. Victim awareness and public acknowledgment add another, vital element. The synergy of information has led to increased recognition of the pervasive and long-term effects of the incestuous relationship. From description and etiology (Courtois & Watts, 1982), we are moving toward diagnosis and treatment paradigms (Faria & Belohlavek, 1984). The parallels between incest and troubled families (Anderson & Shafer, 1979), incest and abuse in general (Goodwin, 1983), incest and post-traumatic stress disorder are being explored (Gelinas, 1983; Goodwin, 1983). In the context of the relationship between incest and other known areas of trouble and coping, then, it may also be appropriate to understand incest from the perspective of the process of mourning and grieving.

Issues of mourning and characteristics of the grieving process are mentioned in the literature on incest (Gelinas, 1983; Sanford, 1984; Wooley & Vigilanti, 1984). Likewise there is recognition that there are tasks which must be accomplished and stages to be gotten through in resolving the effects of incest (Lubell & Soong, 1982; Yassen & Glass, 1984). Effects on the personality of the survivor are acknowledged (Courtois & Watts, 1982). There has not as yet been a detailed description of the incest survivor's characteristic defenses, coping styles, and personality from within the framework of the grieving process.

The process of working through the various stages of mourning the incest experience is complex, convoluted, and far from linear (Courtois & Watts, 1982). It is comprised in part of the developmental stage at which the incest occurred, the defensive style which the child chose to protect herself[1] from and cope with the experience, the degree to which she became able to move through that particular reaction and on to others, and her individual personality.

The stages of mourning can be grouped into two general clusters: those that involve "closing off" (including such characteristics as denial, confusion, and numbness), and those that involve "opening up" to affects (such as anger, guilt, loss and sadness) (Kübler-Ross, 1969; Lindeman, 1944; Slagle, 1982). Are there ways in which the incest survivor can be seen to use or have used these stages—as a child or as an adult? Is this paradigm a valid and useful description of the incest survivor's experience as she works through her traumatic past? What follows is a detailed, first-person description of the mourning process as experienced

---

[1]While there is increasing recognition of male as well as female incest victims, for the present purposes the victim/survivor will be referred to as "she." The preponderance of victims are still female. Further, all clients described here are female. For comparable reasons (general frequency and specific cases), the prepetratrator is here described as "he."

Incest here is defined from a clinical, rather than legal (with all its variants) perspective. Gelinas (1983) suggests that within this framework "incest can be defined by two criteria: sexual contact and a *preexisting* relationship between adult and child" (p. 313).

by a number of incest survivors. Mostly, they are women who are members of a long-term therapy incest-survivors' group. Though they all live in a semirural setting, they vary demographically with regard to age, social class, sexual orientation, and current family structure. Their voices are echoed by others who recount their experiences of these same emotions.

STAGES OF MOURNING

Closing Off

Denial

Childhood experience. Denial is perhaps the most typical, salient characteristic of the incest experience itself (Gelinas, 1983). The perpetrator, the victim, the significant others all tend to deny, albeit from different motives.

The perpetrator generally denies or distorts what he is doing. Heather, for example, was sexually involved with her adored father. She commented:

> Aren't you denying really because the person who did it denies? I feel like I deny it because the person who did it denied it. Because of the denial of the perpetrator, as though it never happened, there's only one choice for a child and that's to deny it too, if the adult involved denies it. You're doing what they're doing—they're showing you by example.

As the incest takes place, many feelings are aroused, including pain, love, identification, and fear. Overwhelming and intolerable as this multitude of affects is, the child not infrequently denies the experience as she is experiencing it (Gelinas, 1983). Heather continued:

> If you think back when you're a child or look at a child who hasn't had anything like this happen and how they look at an adult, you know, it's more than just someone that's responsible and supposed to care for them. That person seems so big, you know—and then when something like this happens, part of you can't believe it. Protection of the particular loved person. Refusing the memory of the person; I feel if I bring it up I'm hurting that person. The feeling I'm needing to protect that person—being responsible for the well-being of my father.

If she tells someone, the person she tells may need to deny the reality (Gutheil & Avery, 1977). Within the family system, the prohibition against knowledge or acknowledgment of the family secret is strong.

Olga confided in her brother, hoping that he might in some way stop her relationship with her uncle. He said nothing, but apparently took her telling him as permission-giving, for he then began coming in to fondle her in her bedroom at night. Olga did not again risk telling her secret for another 15 years.

Adult personality. Incest survivors tend to be emotionally isolated, continuing as adults to see themselves as different, separate from others (Courtois & Watts, 1983; Tsai & Wagner, 1978; Westerlund, undated). The impact is so extensive that it has become part, by now, of who they are. Typical comments include: "I don't tend to make friends easily." "It only happened once." "It was so long ago, I should have gotten over it by now." They may deny the impact or importance of the incest experience (Gelinas, 1983) if not the experience itself. Celia entered therapy with few friends, socially isolated. She described her relationship to others, even those to whom she was beginning to feel close:

> I think sometimes I don't express how much I'm hurt because I don't think other people I'm telling it to—it's almost like I think I'm being—feeling sorry for myself and I don't deserve that much of their sympathy.

The effect of this form of denial is that these women often don't seek help. If they do, it may be for symptoms they see as unrelated to their incest history (Cole, 1984; Courtois & Watts, 1982; Faria & Belohlavek, 1984; Gelinas, 1983). They may be quick to withdraw from therapy. Susan for example, entered treatment because of intractible headaches. When asked during intake about any history of abuse, she mentioned some sexual involvement with her brothers, but quickly added, "It was just neighborhood fooling around." She was unwilling to describe it further, and dropped out of treatment as soon as her headaches abated.

Denial may be used as a defense against memories of the incest experience. Denial can also become a general means of structuring the world. Marge, for example, spoke of ways in which she "erases" parts of her life which feel uncomfortable. In therapy group one week, Olga gave a detailed account of her incest experience. She reported on her reaction the following week:

> It's really hard for me to describe because in a lot of ways I very neatly put last week away. My first impulse was to say: What did I

say last week? Because I didn't really have a bad reaction or anything. I did feel better, I really did, but on the other hand, I can't remember a lot of what went on last week.

Confusion

Closely related to denial is confusion, which occurs when the primitiveness of denial begins to break down. Heather recalled her sense of

> . . . absolute disbelief, confusion, incomprehensibility. Something happened that couldn't have happened. I know something happened but I know it couldn't have happened. And those two—they live together. 'Cause if you say that it actually happened, then you have to—I don't know what you have to do—but the impossible is possible. If what couldn't happen did happen, then you have to learn a whole new way to put everything together. Definitely. So it ends up you did it and you didn't do it. And I end up not having any sense of who I am.

The client may present herself as distracted, unable to attend or focus, confused. Initially, she may see little relation between her confusion and her history. Gelinas (1983) suggests that "the single best indicator of an undisclosed incest victim is the complaint of confusion in a nonpsychotic person" (p. 327).

Numbness

Childhood experience. Like denial, numbness is one of the defenses typically used by the incest victim as she is experiencing the trauma (Gelinas, 1983; Goodwin, 1983). Westerlund reports that "one of the ways in which incest victims cope with their abuse is to numb themselves physically and mentally during the sexual acts" (p. 6).

Adult personality. Numbness is often transmuted into part of the woman's personality style (Gelinas, 1983), so that she operates with a general lack of feeling. Heather asked Olga:

> Did you feel like what you felt when you were a child when you were telling your story? Like the numbness was the kind of feeling you had then? Maybe that's how you stood it then.
> Olga: Yes, in a way. It's like this is the way I'm going to protect myself to get myself through this kind of thing. It's like if you stare at one space a lot of feeling might not come through, and so you can

just say it and it's just like you're going to bring it straight out without a lot of feeling.

Opening Up

Rage/Anger

Childhood experience. Goodwin (1983) cites a number of descriptions of the "maladaptive expression of aggression" (p. 7) in abused children. Lubell and Soong (1982), describing their work with sexually abused adolescents, report that "anger was always present" (p. 313). Anderson and Shafer (1979) describe family members as having major difficulty with impulse control.

Adult personality. Anger about the incest experience is multilayered (Wooley & Vigilanti, 1984). As with other traumas, when unleashed it is often powered by an underlying rage built up and unexpressed over the years (Shatan, 1978). The anger may be in relation to the abuse itself and to the perpetrator. Olga was becoming aware of a multitude of feelings:

> I guess one thing that triggers in my mind—I don't know if it's the anger exactly or what it is—but the realization: somebody hurt me very badly and they took a very important part away from me and they had no right to do that and you can't make it all better. You can't change what happened. That causes me a lot of anger that somebody had the gall to hurt me.

Celia began to feel less isolated as she shared some commonality of affect:

> Well, my feelings are similar to theirs as far as being angry because of what was taken away from me, you know the feeling that he just never had the right to do that and anger and sadness that it had to happen, that it did happen, how big a piece of my life it took out.

Recently, Evy's father (the perpetrator) had a major heart attack. Evy was outraged at the thought that he might die before experiencing a lengthy period of (physical) pain.

There is also a sense of rage that a child (oneself) was molested. Olga continued the tentative exploration of her anger:

> I feel that there's more anger than what I'm letting out. The anger that I can feel and I guess that I can say is that anger towards the— just hurting that child and taking the childhood away from the child.

Anger, ironically, arises in relation to the fall from grace of the powerful figure. Heather articulated this feeling:

> If it's your father or someone you trust completely as being like a god almost, someone who can do no wrong. This person would never hurt me. How can this person who would never hurt me be hurting me?

There may, likewise, be anger and outrage at the failure of some other ostensibly protective figure (typically the mother) to have protected the child: to have prevented the incest from occurring or put a stop to it (Tsai & Wagner, 1978; Wooley & Vigilanti, 1984). Darlene is furious with her mother for not having stopped or prevented the incest. Her mother had in fact asked Darlene if anything was occurring between her and her stepfather. Even though she was aware that her mother had observed the stepfather hugging and kissing her, Darlene said no. She was sure her mother wouldn't want to know. Her mother, she thought, would then have to make a choice between her husband or her children. Darlene expected that she and perhaps her siblings would be sent to live with "Mrs. Meaney," a mythical character her parents had invented with whom to threaten the children. This funneling of denial, projection, displacement, and "parentification," (Gelinas, 1983) into one particular affect—in this case, rage—is illustrative of the complexity and overdetermined character of many responses.

Anger is also felt toward those who deny or don't know. This sense of a separate reality compounds the feelings of being different and isolated. Olga, for example, approached her anger from a new angle: "When I went to my uncle's funeral, I sat there trying to listen to people say how wonderful he was and I just wanted to yell and scream and say, 'No, he wasn't so wonderful.' "

Another variant is the use of anger as a personality style. Susan's headaches were fueled by rage toward her children, husband, and family of origin. Yelling and screaming, which were daily occurrences, merely increased her anger. The anger, for Susan, underlined her belief in herself as an unfriendly person, and, protectively, allowed her to be close to no one.

Anger can become a generalized emotion, applicable to many settings. Heather looked to the group to validate her experience:

> I'd like to ask you something about your feelings of anger and rage. Do you ever experience the anger or rage when you see couples together or when you see relationships—people in relationships—do you find yourself feeling anger towards them for no more reason than perhaps just the fact that they have a relationship? Even my

> own son and his wife—or if I see a movie—say I'm watching a
> movie where people are hugging or kissing. . . .

Anger may be generalized even more, expressed in relation to children
or men in general. Looking at the broader sweep, Heather asked:

> Do you ever feel real angry because it happens to so many children?
> I feel a real anger. It seems like it must be the strongest feeling, the
> hardest because it goes so many different places and ways and how
> it's going on so many times right now, so many children. Many
> people—many men—are not understanding what they are doing to
> those children. That causes an awful lot of anger in me. The trouble
> is it carries over into everybody. It seems like it carries over even if
> you don't want to know it's there, like I keep wanting to say all men
> are the same.

How this aspect of the anger is used varies. For some it is a defense
against looking at one's own anger about one's own experience—a form
of distancing and intellectualization. For others it becomes the impetus to
helping troubled children (personalized) or advocating for decreased sex-
ism (societal).

Guilt/Shame/Survivor Guilt/Bargaining

Childhood experience. One of the most confusing and disturbing
aspects of incest for the child is that she may have experienced physically
pleasurable sensations in conjunction with a variety of other emotions
(Tsai & Wagner, 1978). Westerlund reports that "women with histories
of incest may feel intense shame if they experienced physiological arousal
when stimulated" (p. 6). Celia has been able to describe in some detail
her experience with her brother-in-law, as well as the repugnance she
felt. She had been considerably more reticent about her subsequent sexual
relationship with her uncle. The pleasure she experienced in this latter
relationship has seemed to be a source of shame for her. (The avuncular
relationship has also been the source of uncomfortable flashbacks which
have interfered with her sexual relationship with her husband.)

Survivor guilt is often a component of the person's reaction. In the
power context within which incest frequently occurs, the child traded or
traded on her sexual acquiescence in exchange for some decreased threat
to herself. For Celia, incest with her brother-in-law started after he had
beaten her brother. She was threatened with a beating as well, if she did
not comply with his expectations.

> I really felt bad about my younger brother when the thing happened.
> I think back and he was in the room and the door was shut but I

could hear all the pain he was going through and I just felt so guilty and felt so bad and there was just nothing I could do. He was suffering and I just couldn't help him and that's a guilt and a pain I've carried around that I didn't realize until I started talking about it here.

Bargaining (Kübler-Ross, 1969) is an intrinsic part of the incest experience. The wish to postpone punishment, the "reward" for "being good" are all part of the interaction. This appears true whether the bargain is aimed at decreasing the harm or increasing the benefit to the self. Either way, the incest victim cannot make a bargain without incurring guilt. Olga's poignant description of the bargain was that:

I was getting attention, warmth, love. That was about the only place I felt that was true. That was one of the big things that I rationalized for it to go on. The only other place I felt warmth was when I'd go to the dentist and he'd put his arm around me in order to fill my teeth. After it ended, and the warmth too was gone then there were only negative feelings: anger at him, fear it would start again if I let down my guard, and a feeling of responsibility for everything which had gone on.

Adult personality. The incest survivor, in part because of her role within the family as parentified child (Gelinas, 1983), takes on responsibility for the actions of others as well as herself (Westerlund, undated). Guilt and an attitude of responsibility for what happened become an integral part of her sense of self (Faria & Belohlavek, 1984; Goodwin, 1983; Wooley & Vigilanti, 1984). Even though her father has been dead more than 40 years, Heather continued, in the incest survivor's group, to feel that "if I bring it up I'm hurting my father. I feel awful for even working with it. I feel I'm needing to protect him, that I'm responsible for the well-being of my father." The incest survivor views all interactions as potentially sexualized, and wonders in what ways she is provocative (Yassen & Glass, 1984). Carol said she feared just walking down the street because workmen would whistle at her. Sheila became aware that she had gained a large amount of weight so that the shape of her body would not be apparent.

The incest survivor typically feels isolated and different, with few friends (Faria & Belohlavek, 1984; Tsai & Wagner, 1978). Perhaps beginning with her sense of differentness from her peers, her secret and her shame, the separateness extends into adulthood in a projected fashion. Julia, involved with her father for 5 years, described her isolation:

I don't go to parties much, and when I do I don't know what to say. I feel different from everyone there. I feel like I dress wrong. I don't know how to act, what normal people do. And—I know it's crazy, but—I always think they'll know what happened. So it's just easier not to go, not to get too close to people.

Sadness/Depression

Childhood experience. Depression as a childhood response to incest is not uncommon (Goodwin, 1983); Sanford, 1984). Olga says:

> One of my mother's biggest complaints was that I used to just lay on my bed for long periods of time. I didn't want anyone to disturb me—although I was always conscious to be fine when I was around my family. In high school, I was depressed to the point where I didn't talk in school.

Lubell and Soong (1982) describe the adolescents with whom they worked as mourning the numerous losses in their lives: loss of family; loss of being normal; loss of ease with others; loss of dreams; and loss of innocence.

Adult personality. With the additional perspective of personal history and understanding that adulthood brings, the losses of which the child or adolescent was aware may loom even larger. Heather mourns the child who never had a chance to be who she might have been. She has a sense of the extent of her loss:

> More than my childhood, my sexuality, my personhood—me as a person, as an expressive person—was taken away. My whole creative expression of myself in every way, every form of creative expression, like the core, where it came from, was killed. It was just shut off. It's never been allowed to flow. My life was taken away from me. So I've just been able to be a shell ever since. So I mourn. The biggest mourning is myself I lost.

Generalized depression may be the first signal with which the incest survivor presents herself for help (Faria & Belohlavek, 1984; Gelinas, 1983; Wooley & Vigilanti, 1984). The depression may include somatic symptoms, such as loss of appetite, sleep disturbance, and psychosomatic disease (Courtois & Watts, 1982; Lindemann, 1944; Slagle, 1982). Physical symptoms may reflect in some ways the actual incest experience itself (Sanford, 1984). Carol, for example, plagued with excema, had been fondled extensively during her childhood.

Resolution

From the foregoing descriptions, there is considerable support for the premise that incest survivors share characteristics of those going through the grieving process. At any one time, it appears that a woman may be involved in a number of stages of mourning. She may have used one particular response as a coping method as a child. That style, of vital use to her at a time of trauma, may become a central defense mechanism or personality characteristic as she grows. Alternatively, she may develop defenses or personality patterns involving other characteristics of the mourning process.

The particular styles and levels of mourning a woman uses are not entirely random and capricious. People are likely to move through some "closing off" before they begin "opening up." Similarly, it is unlikely that a person can maintain the invulnerability of numbness as a defense while working through feelings of anger. Nonetheless, there does not seem to be a specific progression through which all people must go. Anger may be a defense against loss; depression may be a means of coping with guilt.

There are times when a reaction or style is useful and serves a purpose. At other points, a particular reaction masks feelings other than those acknowledged. A person may feel stuck in one stage but not yet ready to venture forward, to allow herself to experience new feelings. Olga, in transition, complains about herself:

> I guess I feel like a broken record. I think it's about the third or fourth week in a row that I've felt really upset. I have such a desire to cry and I cannot let the tears come out. I guess I find it frustrating.

The impetus to change comes when the balance shifts: the old style is no longer as effective as it was. It begins to interfere with the person's functioning or aspirations.

> *Olga:* I guess when . . . what comes to my mind is because it's bumping into other aspects of my life and like denial isn't necessarily working anymore.
> *Therapist:* So what's bumping in, the denial or the history? Or the who you are as a result of what happened?
> *Olga:* I guess the result of the image that I've developed of myself through the whole incest experience, that private image, is really bumping in with the public. And instead of having an image here and an image there, that private image wants to let go of some of the bad feelings and wants to move to accept that public self, instead of being at opposite ends of the spectrum. I guess it's just healing—to heal and to realize those different parts and accepting some of the positive and to feel like it's okay.
> *Therapist:* Am I right in thinking that part of what you're feeling is that the numbness, the denial don't work for me anymore and it's

time for me to get on and get beyond that. Something different. (Ya)
For a while it protected me very well but that's not me anymore.
Olga: Right. That I can't live in two totally separate ways. (Because?) I guess because I do want to believe that I am a good person.
And maybe I have to get rid of some of the guilt and the anger and
everything else in order. . . . Just telling myself doesn't cut it. I
don't feel it and I want to feel it.

Even if the known feelings and ways of coping are unpleasant and ineffective, giving them up is difficult (Wooley & Vigilanti, 1984). Contem-
plating moving out into the world, Celia says:

In a way I'm feeling that the sadness and being home to have time to
think about it and stuff doesn't work for me anymore. It's like it's
something you hang onto, but I'm learning that you don't have to if
you want to get on with your life. Although it's been a big part of
your life, you know. It is your past in some ways. It's like losing
something else, too.
Therapist: If you give up the sadness, it's like losing some part of
you also?
Celia: Yes, that's what it feels like. I'm losing some kind of connection that—or letting go. But it's still hard, letting go. Because it's
something real and it's something that's there which you can identify with. Like a security blanket or something.

As she begins exploring the feelings, the woman becomes aware of the
direction in which she's heading. Heather describes her affective layers:

Heather: I feel very . . . grief is what I would feel if I let myself,
but anger is what's there. It's like anger is a protection for me. It
serves many purposes for me.
Therapist: It protects you against—
Heather: Feeling what I need to feel. Experiencing what I need to
feel, which is grief.
Therapist: And what would you be grieving?
Heather: I think what I lost myself, plus for my father and a lot of
things—I don't know. It seems like to get to the grief is the only way
to ever get back what was taken. I'm not sure if it will ever come
back, but anger first, awful guilt, and then you get down to—it
seems like to what's—not that anger isn't real and guilt aren't real,
'cause they are—but it's like grief is this great big well of tears un-
derneath that you have to get to.

Heather moves farther into the process of change, and can reflect further on that change. She recognizes that each individual has her own particular sequence of steps. She adds:

> Perhaps each of the feelings needs to be accepted to move on to the next one. Perhaps I have trouble accepting my anger and so that keeps me there. Perhaps you have trouble accepting or getting beyond the denial, so maybe we need to be able to accept where we are to move on. I feel like they're steps. I feel we need to accept whatever step we're at to move on to whatever the next step is in the healing process.

Olga describes her transition in the following way:

> I always thought I could kick what I want to come out to feel it. And I cannot kick these days. It's like instead of letting it control—it's never going to go away. You can't erase that. I used to think there was some way I was going to make it all go away. Well that's not going to happen, but it's like there comes a time when you don't want it to take control any more. It's like another aspect of you wants control, but it is hard to give it up. It's very unpredictable and it seems like what I'm feeling is I can't tell what's going to happen. That in some respects I don't feel like I have a lot of control. It's not a scary kind of not having control—but I just can't predict what's coming out. Which is sort of exciting and scary at the same time.

Is there ever a final resolution? Using the imagery which opened this article, will all the cotton balls come out, at some point, so that one has a clean, empty jar? It seems unlikely, for at least the following reasons: the type of trauma which incest represents, striking at some of the most basic of developmental issues, such as trust, power, sexuality; the repetitive nature of its occurrence in childhood, when the personality is being formed; problems in developing a trusting relationship, even in therapy, which make a consistent therapeutic alliance an exceptionally arduous challenge for client and therapist alike.

What, then, can one expect? Amanda shares her realistic, yet hopeful perspective:

> I really don't think it ever disappears. You learn to cope. My brother continues to talk to me about his girlfriends. I don't like hearing him talk about them, and I'm aware of it. The biggest thing is that I now have control over my feelings and can set boundaries and not feel guilty about saying, "I don't want to hear about your

love life.'' I'm not going to be threatened and victimized. He has to respect my boundaries. I have to take responsibility for verbalizing them. But knowing that I have control, that I'm aware of my feelings means that I now can rebound from situations which used to devastate me for days.

REFERENCES

Anderson, L.M., & Shafer, G. (1979). The character-disordered family: A community treatment model for family sexual abuse. *American Journal of Orthopsychiatry. 49* (3), 436-445.

Cole, P.M. (1984, August). *Father-daughter incest: Its relationship with victims' own parental attitudes.* Poster presentation at the Annual Meeting of the American Psychological Association, Toronto, Canada.

Courtois, C.A., & Watts, D.L. (1980). Counseling adult women who experienced incest in childhood or adolescence. *The Personnel and Guidance Journal, 60,* 275-279.

Faria, G., & Belohlavek, N. (1984). Treating female survivors of childhood incest. *Social Casework, 65*(8), 465-471.

Gelinas, D. (1983). The persisting negative effects of incest. *Psychiatry, 46,* 312-332.

Goodwin, J. (1983, October). *Posttraumatic symptoms in abused children.* Paper presented at the 11th Annual Friends Hospital Clinical Conference, Philadelphia.

Gutheil, T.G., & Avery, N.C. (1977). Multiple overt incest as family defense against loss. *Family Process, 16*(1), 105-116.

Kübler-Ross, E. (1969). *On death and dying.* New York: Macmillan.

Lindemann, E. (1944). Symptomatology and management of acute grief. *American Journal of Psychiatry, 101,* 141-148.

Lubell, D., & Soong, W.-T. (1982). Group therapy with sexually abused adolescents. *Canadian Journal of Psychiatry, 27,* 311-315.

Sanford, L. (1984, June). Community-based intervention. In *The treatment of child sexual assault: Children and their families.* Workshop in Concord, New Hampshire.

Shatan, C.F. (1978). Stress disorders among Vietnam veterans: The emotional context of combat continues. In C.R. Figley (Ed.) *Stress disorders among Vietnam veterans: Theory, research and treatment* (pp. 43-52). New York: Bruner-Mazel.

Slagle, K. (1982). *Live with loss.* Englewood Cliffs, NJ: Prentice-Hall.

Tsai, M., & Wagner, N.N. (1978). Therapy groups for women sexually molested as children. *Archives of Sexual Behavior, 7,* (5), 417-427.

Westerlund, E. (undated). *Counseling women with histories of incest.* Available from Incest Resources, Inc., Cambridge Women's Center, 46 Pleasant St. Cambridge, MA 02139.

Wooley, M.J., & Vigilanti, M.A. (1984). Psychological separation and the sexual abuse victim. *Psychotherapy, 21*(3), 347-352.

Yassen, J., & Glass, L. (1984). Sexual assault survivors groups: A feminist practic perspective. *Social Work, 29*(3), 252-257.

Grief and Therapy:
Two Processes in Interaction

Jane A. Kamm

ABSTRACT. After correlating grief with pregnancy, the author concentrates on stages in grieving, i.e., denial, anger, guilt, reluctant acceptance, preoccupation with one's own mortality, identification, loneliness, physical symptoms, anniversaries, and finally letting go. Several cogent therapeutic suggestions are offered.

INTRODUCTION

In important ways, grief is similar to pregnancy: (1) It happens to a normal person, (2) starts with a single event, (3) develops into a process, (4) which is inexorable, (5) and accompanied by suffering, (6) but the outcome of which is time-limited, (7) and benign; (8) and the prognosis is excellent.

Patients who are grieving are not necessarily otherwise in need of therapy, but believe that there must be some pathological trait in themselves because the pain is so long and so intense, and they find themselves helpless to stop it. It is probably a mistake to treat grief as an illness that needs to be either overcome or suppressed; in my opinion, drugs merely interfere with and prolong the process of mastering the tragedy. However, as in obstetrics, in treating such a patient there are therapeutic interventions that are appropriate to the patient's present condition, which will enable one to proceed to the next level of working-through. In this paper, the grieving process is described, along with the helpful responses that appear to keep the process moving toward its inevitable and desired conclusion.

STAGES IN GRIEVING

Denial

Therapists usually do not get a patient in the earliest stages of grief, the initial shock and the denial that follows. However, these stages are usual-

Jane A. Kamm, D.S.W., is a psychiatric social worker, in the private practice of psychotherapy in Southfield and Birmingham, Michigan. 17520 West 12 Mile Rd., Southfield, MI 48076.

59

ly described subsequently in therapy hours. What enables one to cope with autopsies, death certificates, writing obituaries and eulogies, funeral arrangements, dealing with relatives, is a kind of numbing out, or a delaying of emotional response—"Not now, later, when everything has been done and I am alone." If one has to deal with lawyers, wills, probate court, it is possible to delay the mourning for quite some time. One goes through the motions, does the right things, makes the necessary decisions, with emotions held in abeyance. Often there is another mechanism that is also operative at first, a denial of the reality of the death—"She has merely gone to the hospital again," "He is just away on a trip." The dead one is still referred to in the present tense. Eventually, reality sets in when one "sits down to write Mother a letter," or tries to telephone, only to realize there will be no answer—ever again. It is at this point that patients begin to think of getting help for themselves, because they are not prepared to deal alone with the startling fury that then arises.

Anger

There is an old folk admonition, "One does not speak ill of the dead." In truth, one does, and one feels ashamed of it. Probably the first reaction is a devastating acknowledgment of one's own personal loss, "How dare you go away and leave me all alone?" This is followed by awareness of the big hole left in the social network by death, with added responsibilities now devolving on surviving members. "How dare you just take off, leaving me to finish raising your family?" "How dare you die with no provision for your own final expenses?" And then one is tormented, often for weeks, with painful memories of every mean, unkind, thoughtless action that the dead person ever perpetrated, and one's own self-questioning: "What a horrible person I must be to remember these things when she suffered so much from cancer." The therapeutic intervention needs to be assurance that this is a temporary, normal stage in mourning; and to encourage complete expression by a form of homework, that a list be made of all the outrageous memories. Once they are thought out, written down, handed in, and talked about completely, they can then be laid aside.

Guilt

In the midst of anger at the dead person, there is also anger at oneself, and guilt. "If only I had done this, had not done that, had tried harder, had tried more things . . . , I could have saved her." Some instruction on omnipotence as a futile illusion is useful here. The nature of the death is often looked at closely by the patient, with the stunning realization of how much the dying person had actually participated in and speeded up his or her own demise. This is usually clear in cases of suicide and also of murder; but as the dying process is studied closely in every detail, the participation of every dead person in his or her own passing becomes quite clear—an unhealthy life-style, admonitions ignored, medication not taken, doctor's orders not complied with, hospital meals not eaten, tubes pulled out, and so on. The end of guilt is a deep personal acceptance of one's own helplessness, and of everybody's right to self-determination: responsibility not only for one's own living, but also for one's own dying. Someone once remarked that no one dies until one is ready to go. We know as the dying person moves closer toward passing, there is an acceptance of the process, indeed a final looking forward to it. If the patient has been fortunate enough to have been able to spend hours talking to the deceased before the event, there will have been some awareness of the eager anticipation of the transition. And as this is recognized and each person's own accountability for his or her own actions is accepted, resignation begins to come. "I guess if my father had wanted to go to live in Hawaii, I would have gladly helped him pack his bags, taken him down to the airport and waved him off."

Reluctant Acceptance

Many patients report dreams in which the dead play an important part. These dreams mirror the stage of mourning that is being currently worked on—at one point still alive on earth, again struggling to leave the dreamer, and then often a dream of the departed person's happy reunion with old friends or relatives but in a foreign land. It helps to ask about any beliefs in the nature of afterlife or in reincarnation. "Where do you think your mother is right now, and what do you imagine she might be doing?" If there is no comforting philosophical belief system, it is often useful to talk about some of the research that has been done on near-death experiences.

Preoccupation With Own Mortality

Every death leads to an awareness of one's own mortality as well. "Is my sister really dead, or is it just that her body has been discarded? What has happened to her unique personality, the part I loved? Was she always just a body, or was she really something else? And what does that mean about me?" One therapist gave a brief lecture on the laws of thermodynamics, bringing the patient to an awareness of personal infinity with the assurance that matter can be neither created nor destroyed. Another's approach was to quote John Quincy Adams who once stated that he himself was very well but the house he was living in was becoming very decrepit and he might soon have to move out and find another abode.

Identification

One way survivors have of maintaining a closeness with the departed is a temporary resort to identification: the wearing of the deceased's clothes or jewelry, the assumption of mannerisms, the taking over of hobbies, occupation, and/or the completion of unfinished tasks (household maintenance, gardening, sewing, community involvement). This is quite helpful when done with awareness. It leads to an appreciation of the benefits of having known the departed and the knowledge that that person lives on inside oneself and in others.

Loneliness

It appears that only as the reality and finality of the death is accepted is it possible for survivors to let themselves experience their loneliness. By that time, all the friends and relatives have returned to their own homes, and one is left to rebuild a shattered life. This is particularly painful in the case of the widowed, with years of living side by side and myriad mutual habits. The death of a spouse is probably one of the most stressful events in any life, particularly if the partners have been very close and communicative. Probably better sooner than later, drawers and closets have to be cleared out: clothes have to be sorted, cleaned, given away; toilet articles thrown out; photographs and letters put away out of sight. One widow spent the entire first year reading through her husband's love-letters to her, fantasizing that he was speaking to her. It was comforting to her but in a way prolonged the acceptance of reality. There is a need for the therapist to encourage reaching out to other people for friendship—someone to talk to and confide in, someone to help with those aspects of living formerly assumed by the dead partner. One of the painful aspects of the readjustment of the widowed is the need for new friends, others who are also unattached, because most widowed feel like fifth wheels among couples. For those left with children, Parents-Without-Partners is a helpful organization. Many widowed may start dating rather quickly with the hope that sexual activity will lessen their distress, only to find that it merely highlights the loss of companionship they are now experiencing. At times there is the expectation that the new person will be exactly like the one who has died, often going as far as to call the new love by the old love's name. Since no one is completely like another, these expectations are bound to lead to disappointment.

The question of moving away often arises, because one's home and one's community are so full of painful memories. However a move is also a stressful event and to leave one's support system is like cutting one's lifeline. Survivors should be encouraged to wait at least a year before they make any moves outside their present familiar environment.

Physical Symptoms

During the first year, survivors often experience physical illness. Many times it resembles the final illness of the person who has died—for example, a mother will die of a breast cancer and shortly thereafter her daughter might develop a breast cyst. However, unrelated physical symptoms also appear that can only be interpreted as the body's response to prolonged stress. At this juncture, concentration on stress-management techniques is helpful: relaxation, meditation, yoga, biofeedback, or hypnosis.

Anniversaries

What has been discussed up to this point is what can be normally expected during the first year of mourning. During this year also, anniversaries are very poignant: the first Thanksgiving without Mother's turkey; the first Christmas not spent at Grandpa's house; the dead person's birthday; the just-missed 50th anniversary; Mother's Day or Father's Day. But there are other anniversaries that are more personal and more painful—"A year ago today, they found Mother's cancer"; "A year ago today, she went to the hospital for the last time"; "A year ago today, she fell into a coma"; "A year ago today, the doctors cut off the life-support systems"; and—the most searing of all, "A year ago today, she passed away in her sleep." Anniversary reactions leave the impression that the past event is now happening for the first time. The caring for a dying person requires decisions to be made, actions to be taken, arrangements, telephone calls, assembling of the clan; and one responds to the demands of reality by a steeling of the nerves. A year later, in the reliving of the tragic events, the appropriate feelings are allowed to come through, often overwhelmingly.

Letting Go

Patients at this point often question whether they are any better, since they are again so overcome by emotion. It is helpful for the therapist to have a mental model of the grieving process and to be able to explain it to the patient, because from this point on, rapid improvement will be made. There is now a need for some form of ritual to signify one's willingness finally really to let go. In some ethnic groups, detailed pictures might have been taken at the funeral, or a tape recording might have been made of the memorial service; and these may be brought out again and reexperienced. Some patients may choose to read aloud from a religious service for the dead during a given therapy session. In other instances, what seems to be required is the two-chair technique involving a confrontation with a final saying good-bye. Again, this may heighten the realization of how much of the departed has been incorporated.

Accompanying the realization of how the dead continue to influence the social structure, comes a shift in the family equilibrium, with everybody in a slightly different role. One patient remarked, "With Daddy's passing, I realized that there are no more old people left in our family; and then I saw that, yes, there are, and my generation is it!"

RECONSTRUCTION

Social customs aside, the first-year anniversary marks the turning point in the grieving process. There will always be an emotional scar. Yet, in many ways, the patient has grown stronger: has experienced dependency, developed independence, and worked through the host of negative feelings about the dead person. If this has been thorough, the grieving person is free to move on to new relationships without the burden of a great deal of emotional carry-over.

A reintroduction into the single life for the widowed may come as a shock. It may not be possible for all widows to remarry, but meaningful relationships and supporting friendships are certainly to be encouraged. The development of new interests and activities will bring that person into contact with people of like concerns. Particularly as one becomes involved in service organizations, there is a transcendence as the individual feels useful to others, and with that comes contentment and eventually happiness.

It is certainly worth while to encourage patients to remember all the things they used to say they always wanted to do but never had the time or the money, or felt free enough, to pursue—travel, more education, cultural activities, sports, a new business. The death of one's life-partner need not be the end of things but a chance for a new beginning. Especially where the relationship with a spouse has been very close and cherished, the guilt of enjoying oneself is surplanted by the realization that those in love want their partners to continue to be happy. Eventually, the daily grieving at the gravesite must end; the sunshine begins to be seen, the song of the birds is heard again. With renewed courage, one picks up the pieces of one's existence, and life moves on.

A Gestalt Therapist's Perspective on Grief

Edward W. L. Smith

ABSTRACT. Reflecting on Freud's approach to mourning and melancholia, the author first distinguishes grief from depression. He then suggests a three-dimensional schema involving the intensity, duration, and type of loss involved in the grieving process. Attending to the highly variable nature of this process, he describes grieving or "mourning labor" as the organism's natural healing process whereby the loss is acknowledged and the organism is made ready to go on with life, unaccompanied by that which was let go. The role of the therapist is seen as one of facilitating the natural individualized process of grieving. Help is most appropriate when the client is unable to grieve or has been grieving too long. In the first case the client is seen as refusing to enter into the experience of the labor of mourning and in the latter as refusing to finish the work. The article concludes with a description of the "empty-chair monologue" in which the client is encouraged to do the mourning labor of expressing appreciations, resentments, and regrets while the therapist attends to any inadequacy of awareness, of arousal, or of crying activity.

Sorrow comes as a welcome visitor,
moving my losses to the archives of my life.
But, depression is her monstrous half-sister
wanting to be a murderous wife.

One of the frequent confusions in this bizarre realm known by the misleading name of "mental health" is the confusion of grief with depression. In the attempt to simplify, make it easy, and, in turn, popularize psychology, there is often a failure to differentiate the natural process of grieving a loss from the neurotic process, depression. The confusion is easy for the merchant of oversimplification, since, when viewed superficially, grief and depression bear resemblance. But, to consent to this superficiality is to lose the profoundly important distinction between these two human processes.

Allow me the following analogy. In the latter half of the 19th century

Edward W. L. Smith, Ph.D., is in full-time independent practice of psychotherapy and does psychotherapy training in Atlanta. He is editor of *The Growing Edge of Gestalt Therapy*. His mailing address is: 1145 Sheridan Road N.E., Atlanta, GA 30324.

the Augustinian monk Gregor Mendel revealed to the world the basic answers to the enigma of heredity. In his Moravian gardens Mendel was able to show predictable outcomes in his selective breeding of peas. But a riddle arose. When crossing two hybrid plants the ratio of the observable characteristics in the offspring was 3:1, not half and half, as one might expect. Through painstaking, countless trials Mendel observed until he solved the riddle. Like appearance does not reveal underlying genetic make-up. Or, phenotypic identity (same physical appearance) does not necessitate the same genotype (actual gene content). Only by getting to the level of genotype, with its 1:2:1 ratio of inheritance of a given genetically carried characteristic, was Mendel able to solve the riddle of the 3:1 ratio in the appearance of that characteristic (the phenotype). Appearances presented a riddle, and the solution came through an understanding of the underlying process.

So it is, too, for the psychotherapist. Beneath the phenotype layer of crying and sad talk lie two distinct genotypes, grief and depression. These two processes are different in quite significant ways, as I shall review shortly. And, to treat grieving and depression in the same manner is wasteful at best; at worst, it is of real harm to the patient. How often is the grieving patient treated as depressed, or the depressed patient treated as if grieving?

I feel concerned with the blurring of the distinction between grief and depression that I read with some frequency in the literature and hear from psychotherapists. Such blurring of categories is at variance with a basic value in Gestalt therapy. Fritz Perls studied with the Organismic theorist Kurt Goldstein, learning from him the value of care in speaking. Goldstein emphasized the importance of the ability of the person to abstract and classify, thereby engaging in "categorical thinking." He was able to demonstrate that the loss of categorical thinking by patients resulted in limitations of their orientation and of their action. Following Goldstein's lead, Perls pointed out throughout his writing the extreme importance of using the words which express the precise meaning of what one wants to convey. He encouraged the appreciation of the power in the "logos," the valuing of each word with its precise meaning and application in communication (Emerson & Smith, 1974). The study of semantics was encouraged by Perls (1947, 1969) as an excellent method of improving mental functioning and as the antidote to what he poetically referred to as "frigidity of the palate." So, once again, I want to emphasize the importance of speaking precisely when we speak of grief or depression, for both clarity of understanding and the ensuing guidelines to therapeutic practice.

Just as Mendel looked beneath appearances to understand the genotypes unrevealed through phenotype, Freud looked beneath the surface behaviors to understand the two processes referred to in the words of his time as "mourning" and "melancholia." Although there are earlier references in which the comparison of these two dynamics was made, such as that of Abraham in 1912, the classic article was published by Freud in 1917, titled simply "Mourning and Melancholia" (Freud, 1963).

Freud instructed that it was the same kinds of external events that brought about mourning or melancholia. The key to the onset of either is an experienced loss. The loss is, in Freud's words, "of a loved person, or the loss of some abstraction which has taken the place of one, such as fatherland, liberty, an ideal, and so on" (p. 164). For some, having "morbid pathological dispostion," instead of mourning, a state of melancholia ensues. In both cases there is the experience of "profoundly painful dejection, abrogation of interest in the outside world, loss of the capacity of love, inhibition of all activity" (p. 165). In the case of melancholia, however, there is in addition "a lowering of the self-regarding feelings to a degree that finds utterance in self-reproaches and self-revilings, and culminates in a delusional expectation of punishment" (p. 165). It is this that is the *differentia specifica* at the symptomatic level, between mourning and melancholia—the fall in self-esteem.

My focus, here, is on grieving, as mourning is also called, not on melancholia, now more frequently termed depression. So I shall not look further into the theories and research that have clarified the "morbid pathological disposition" which is the etiological key to depression, as opposed to grieving. I want to shift focus now to grieving, by first quoting Rycroft (1968) as saying, "All schools of psychoanalysis regard mourning as the normal analogue of DEPRESSION (sic)" (p. 94).

I have made a case for the importance of a differential diagnosis between grief and depression. As old as the distinction is, the boundary is often blurred or ignored even by professionals. So, how is grieving identified? Freud, as discussed above, pointed the way. In grieving, a loss has been sustained. If the grieving is progressing smoothly, the affected person will feel a level of sadness and withdrawal of interest and activity from the world that is congruent with the degree of loss. What will not be present is the loss of self-esteem that characterizes depression. There may be regrets, of course. But these regrets remain just that. In loss, I may regret that I did not go to see the deceased during his or her illness; I may regret that there are some things that I never said. But, in clean grieving I would not call myself a bad person for not having done those things. To elaborate on the recognition of grieving, there are some subtleties that I want to mention. Sadness and withdrawal of interest and activity may manifest in a rich panorama of mourning. Included may be feelings of emptiness, pessimism, and despair. There may be crying, in all degrees from tearing up or sniffling to deep, long wailing. The person in grief may feel fatigued, with everything seeming to require great effort. With this lowered level of energy, speech and movement may be slowed, concentration may be difficult, and the person may become error-prone as attention is hard to keep. Sleep may come only with difficulty, compounding the problem of fatigue and perhaps leading to general irritability. Appetite fails. And, sexual drive usually reaches its nadir. The intensity and duration of these manifestations is dictated by the degree of experienced loss.

What, then, constitutes loss? Freud's (1963) suggestion that the loss may be of a loved person or of some abstraction which has taken the place of a loved person is, once again, an astute guide, and one deserving elaboration. The human ability to abstract the person, then abstract the abstraction, can lead to a final object with emotional attachment which is not at all apparent to the observer. So, there are grief reactions to losses which go unnoticed by those other than the one involved. A list of losses, categorized as Obvious Losses, Not So Obvious Losses, Losses Related to Age, Limbo, and Other Losses (temporary losses, losses built into successes, mini-losses), offered by Colgrove, Bloomfield, and McWilliams (1976) runs fully two pages. I shall pass on to you some selected examples to give a flavor, and to bring out some of their less obvious examples: death of a loved one, divorce, break-up of an affair, loss of money, illness (loss of health), robbery, loss of a cherished ideal, loss of childhood dreams, leaving home, graduating, loss of hair or teeth, awaiting medical test reports, a loved one "missing in action," slump in business, children away at college, a dent in the new car. The point which these authors make is that these losses, whether immediate or cumulative, sudden or eventual, obvious or subtle, create an emotional wound or injury to the organism.

As I have thought about loss I have envisioned a three-dimensional schema. The first dimension is twofold, representing gradual loss and sudden loss. The second dimension is fourfold, and represents the type of loss—person, animal, object, idea. The third dimension is one of intensity and is best thought of as a continuum from slight loss to extreme loss. I want to explore these dimensions. Whereas gradual loss is itself a continuum of time, sudden loss is clearly distinct as a psychological experience. Allow me to clarify. Gradual losses are experienced over a period of time, be it years, months, weeks, days, or even shorter. But in any case, the person experiences a gradualness of the loss, or the warning of the loss over a period of time. For example, one may watch the decline of a home neighborhood over a period of years as population shifts and rezoning take their effect. Or, one may receive notice of condemnation of one's home property for the building of a new highway, the eviction date being several months hence. In each of these two cases there is a gradualness of the loss, either through a progressiveness of the loss or an advanced warning of the loss. With such gradualness of loss there may be an extended period of grieving, perhaps with periods of "time out" during which the person goes on about life as if the loss were not occurring, only to return to another episode in the overall grieving process. With prolonged gradual loss there may also be a wearing down and fatiguing of the grieved, the process which in Spanish is termed "cansar." When, on the other hand, the loss is sudden, there is a shock reaction. With shock there may be a period of disbelief or denial, and a feeling of numbness. As the shock subsides the other feelings of grief take over.

Turning, now, to the types of loss, the category of "person" includes all losses in relationship, some of which were mentioned above. The important thing to remember is that *any* relationship with another person that is subjectively felt can be lost, and with that loss grief can be experienced. "Animal" is an interesting category in that pets are treated in many respects like humans by their owners, but that private relationship may not be recognized by the outsider. And, obviously, the person and animal categories share the quality of being relationships with other life.

Relationships with nonliving objects can take on rich symbolic meaning and can be of considerable intensity. Whether the home neighborhood of the above example, a personal car, an old jacket, or a pocket knife handed down from one's father, the object may be cherished to a greater or lessor degree, and thereby become a source for the experience of loss.

The fourth category for loss, "ideas," contains several things. What is common among them is that they are nonmaterial entities with which one may relate. Oftentimes these relationships with things mentalistic are quite private, so outsiders may not recognize easily when a loss has taken place. By ideas I mean one's hopes, dreams, plans, and illusions. Whenever a hope is dashed, a dream disappears, a plan fails, or the bubble of illusion is burst by an undeniable prick of reality, a loss is sustained. As I write this a scene from my boyhood comes back vividly. I remember in fourth grade watching the boy who was believed by all of the other boys, as well as by himself, to be the fastest runner, stand in tears at the end of a race in which someone had outrun him. His myth had been shattered. From so simple an example as this, to complex examples of lifelong dreams, the losses are real and demand a proper grieving.

The third dimension of my schema is concerned with the magnitude or intensity of loss. The important thing to recognize about this dimension is that the experience of loss is highly subjective, so that what for one person might be only a slight loss, for another that loss might be devastating. The crucial factor is the degree of relationship felt. As the saying goes, you can't lose what you never had.

For clarity, a two-dimensional drawing of my schema appears in Figure 1.

The message of my three-dimensional schema is that loss comes in myriad form. The implication of that message is that the grieving process

Figure 1.

Schema of Loss

	Person	Animal	Object	Idea
Sudden				
Gradual				

which ensues is highly variable in its intensity, its duration, and its style. Although there is a set of feelings, as presented above, which are recognized as the feelings of mourning, there is no set pattern for grief.

Grieving, or as Freud called it, the "mourning labor," is the organism's natural healing process whereby the loss is acknowledged and the organism is made ready to go on with life, unaccompanied by that which was let go. The organism withdraws from the world, in grief, and into itself in order to feel keenly the loss and to access its meaning. Grief is a natural and powerful figure that can emerge with such clarity and vividness that all else is but a vague background. The everydayness of life has importance only as an irritant, distracting from the healing at hand. This process is to be respected. As Freud (1963) acknowledged, "we look upon any interference with it as inadvisable or even harmful" (p. 165).

Clearly, then, the role of the therapist is to facilitate the natural individualized process of grieving, and not to prevent it, interfere with it, or short–circuit it. There are two situations in which a therapist is of special help in grieving. One is the situation in which the person who has sustained loss seems unable to grieve. The other is the case of grief which seems to be going on too long.

When someone has obviously suffered a significant loss, and yet does not grieve, I think in terms of two dynamics which may be operating, singularly or together. The first is *pain phobia.* Perls (1969, 1975) identified the "phobic attitude" of the neurotic, and more specifically, the phobic attitude toward pain. Perls (1969) placed great emphasis on the phobic attitude, which he also termed the "avoidance" and the "flight from." In his words, "The enemy of development is the pain phobia—the unwillingness to do a tiny bit of suffering" (p. 56). In the case of deep grief, the suffering is more than "a tiny bit," of course. But, the point is that the avoidance of feeling pain is a way of trying to sidestep part of life. Losses demand grieving, a feeling of the loss, and a hurting with the loss in order to let go and move on with life. To refuse to do the hurting, to refuse to fully feel and express the sadness is to interrupt a natural organismic process and thereby create "unfinished business." I am struck with how often patients want me to take away the pain of their grief, to help them avoid the hurt and the tears. Sometimes they even believe that their sadness and their tears are evidence that they are neurotic. The pain phobia, the fear of natural psychological pain, is sometimes culturally supported and a part of the illusion that when one gets far enough along in therapy there will be no more pain. This is the "self-image actualization" myth. As Perls noted, nature has created pain in order to call attention to something important. In grief, attention is being called to the loss, the importance of the processing of that loss. By staying with the unpleasantness, rather than running from it, one can move through it and feel a completion of the process of grief.

The second dynamic which can prevent grieving fully is the "be strong" script. The wording varies, including such messages as "Don't be weak," "Don't cry," "Don't show your emotions," "Don't show you're hurt," and "Be a man." Messages such as these all have as their essential meaning, "you should be strong," and imply that to feel sad and to cry, and otherwise to express sadness, is a sign of weakness. In *The Body in Psychotherapy* (Smith, 1985, ch. 3) I described the process of taking in toxic script messages as follows:

> The treatment of the child by the parents, in general or in specific ways, encourages natural aliveness or discourages or even forbids it. During early development, most importantly the first five years or so, children are told not to express a certain feeling in a particular way, or not to express that feeling at all, or not to feel that feeling, or not to get excited, or sometimes not even to have certain wants. These prohibitive messages may be expressed verbally or non-verbally. Due primarily to the profound dependence of the child on the parenting figures for its very survival, the prohibitive messages are "swallowed whole," introjected. Secondarily, the process of introjection is facilitated by the fact that the child has little life experience, relative to the parenting figures, against which to judge the prohibitive messages. During this phase of the socialization process, many of the introjected messages are bionegative, that is, they are socially arbitrary messages which do not support the child's aliveness. The bionegative message is, then, a Toxic Introject.
>
> There are two components to the Toxic Introject. First, is the content, or the specific prohibition. Second, is the threat that if the Toxic Introject is not obeyed love will be denied. The threat is ex-

perienced as if something awful, terrible, even catastrophic will happen. An example is the message to a little boy, "Big boys don't cry. Don't be a sissy." The content of this message is, "You should not cry," and the threat is, "If you cry I won't love you any more." Such Toxic Introjects are usually maintained, unexamined and unchallenged, throughout one's life. The result is lifelong internal conflict between the natural urge for aliveness and the toxic, introjected message which calls for deadness. Once the toxic message has been introjected, the threat of loss of love for disobeying becomes a conditioned phobic belief in imminent catastrophe whenever the toxic message is not honored. The Toxic Introject carries a "should" or "should not" (the content) and a Catastrophic Expectation.

As an aside, I want to mention a couple of common phrases which carry the meaning of "Be strong." The existence of these as highly recognizable sayings gives evidence for the pervasiveness of the "be strong" script in our culture. One phrase is "Chin up!" The other is to "Keep a stiff upper lip." The latter has been traced to John Easter in 1833 (Sperling, 1981). "What's the use of boohooin? Keep a stiff upper lip, no bones broke—don't I know?" (p. 28). The phrase "a stiff upper lip" has come to mean an unfeeling person.

Notice that both of these dynamics which prevent full grieving are based on phobic behavior. In one case there is a pain phobia, and in the other case there is a phobia of breaking an old toxic–script message. That latter phobia is what is otherwise termed the "catastrophic expectation."

The experience of loss sets up a state of tension. It is through grieving that this tension is relieved. Therefore, the absence of full grieving results in "unfinished business," an incompleted task. To the extent that the task of grieving is not complete the person suffering loss is left in a state of some degree of tension. It is a law of human nature that things don't just go away, and, contrary to the platitude, time does not heal all. What heals the wound of loss is grieving the loss. Grieving takes time, and that may be the source of the platitude. What is important, though, is what one is doing by way of mourning labor during the passage of time.

When grieving is avoided, the unfinished business remains forever. With effort the grief can be kept from awareness much of the time. But it is still there, the tension ready to break into awareness whenever the rigid vigil is not kept. The clinical evidence for this dynamic of unfinished business is compelling. A dramatic example from my own experience is a woman I worked with briefly several years ago. Her father had died 20 some years before, and she had never grieved. In the workshop she told of how she had read comic books in the limousine on the way to the cemetery so as to keep herself away from the funeral experience and to appear to everyone as unmoved by her father's death. For all these years she had maintained her nongrieving position, of course having to rigidify her life and limit her exposure to reminders of "father" and of "death." In the workshop she asked for help in grieving, wanting to be able to expand her living beyond the narrowed limits which she had had to observe. My co-therapist and I created a casket from some pillows, and invited her to see her deceased father lying in state. As she imaged this scene she gradually began to weep. We encouraged her talking to him, her expressing her long-guarded feelings toward him. After a few minutes of talking to him and weeping, she exploded into deep wailing. Her crying continued for almost an hour, as we held her. I had never before witnessed so dramatic an example of giving into the process of grieving after an extended period of the refusal to grieve.

Turning, now, to the second situation in which a therapist can be of use in the grief process, we find an undue prolongation of grieving. Whereas the absence of full grieving *creates* unfinished business, the prolonging of grieving *maintains* a condition of unfinished business. In the former case there is a refusal to fully enter into and experience the labor of mourning. The latter case consists of a refusal to finish the work, to let go and move on with one's life.

There are, I believe, two dynamics which may extend the grieving period beyond what is natural. First, grief may feed an underlying depression. If one is characterologically disposed to depression, then the labor of mourning may serve to introduce the dysphoria and to set off a depressive episode. Since the symptoms of mourning match those of depression, except for the fall in self-esteem in the latter case, it is an easy transition for the predisposed person to use a loss as an entrée to depression. Tears of grief and tears of depression both are wet and salty.

The second dynamic which may extend the period of grieving is akin to the psychoanalytic concept of "secondary gain." If the labor of mourning is more exciting than the alternatives seen in one's life, then the mourning may go on indefinitely. Mourning labor has its own reason and dynamic, but secondarily, entering into the process may provide meaning to an otherwise drab existence. The increase in meaning may come from a sense of focus and importance of the mourning labor, as well as increased attention from others. So, one may make a fetish of one's grieving, and then be reluctant to allow it to come to completion.

Figure 2 summarizes these situations in which the natural process of grieving is diverted and therapeutic intervention is helpful.

To emphasize the point again, grieving, appropriate to the loss experienced, is necessary for healthy living to go on. Without grieving, the person who has sustained loss is tied to the past by her or his unfinished business. As Perls (1947, 1969) wrote, "Mourning is a part of the resignation process, necessary if one is to overcome the clinging to the past. This process called 'mourning labour' is one of the most ingenious discoveries of

Figure 2

Therapeutic Intervention in Grieving

I. Absence of full grieving (Creates "unfinished business")

        A. Pain phobia

        B. "Be strong" script.

II. Undue prolongation of grieving (Maintains "unfinished business")

        A. Grief feeding underlying depression.

        B. Grief as a major source of meaning in life.

Freud'' (pp. 96-97). Interestingly, Perls observed that in the analysis of the retrospective character (the person obsessed with the past) there is always one distinct symptom—the suppression of crying. So, to suppress the labor of mourning is to invest in the past, and rob the present.

So what is the nature of grief? In Macbeth (IV.iii) Shakespeare offers us the observation, and warning:

> Give sorrow words; the grief that
> > does not speak
> Whispers the o'er fraught heart and
> > bids it break.

Not only is Shakespeare acknowledging the need for grieving, anticipating Freud's discussion of mourning labor and Perl's expressive methods, but he is calling attention to the "heaviness" of sorrow. Indeed, our word "grieve" derives from the Latin "gravare" meaning to burden, to oppress. That Latin verb relates to the adjective "gravis," or "heavy," from which we have evolved the word "gravity." So, we are informed etymologically that grief is heavy. It can burden and oppress with its gravity, and if not given words, as Shakespeare at once advises and warns, may break the heart. Allowing further etymological elucidation of grief, we can turn to the synonym "sorrow." Here we find the Middle English "sorwe" and the Anglo-Saxon "sorg" as roots, and a new meaning in Scottish and Irish use. In those countries "sorrow" also means the devil! Another dimension is added if we look at some names which involve the word "mourning." The "mourning widow" known also as the "mourning bride" is a garden plant having dark purple flowers. A purplish-brown wing is found on the butterfly known as the "mourning cloak." And, the "mourning warbler" has a breast of black. The darkness—purple, brown, black—earned each of these their "mourning" epithet. Those who bestowed the names recognized the relationship of darkness and grief, and by the same symbolic connection chose black as the non-color for the "mourning band" to be worn on the mourner's arm. Finally, there is the "mourning dove" which gives us a sound by which to understand the meaning of grief. Informed, then, by the sound, the color, and the logos, we know something of the nature of grief. Heavy, burdening, oppressive, grave. Brown, purple, black, dark. A sound which is low, and repeated in a slow rhythm, reaching deeply inside and pulling a sadness. An encounter with something from hell! So powerful can be the experience, that we can identify grief with God, and at the same time call upon Him. I base this on the fact of the use of the expletive "Good grief!" as a minced form of the oath "Good God!" (Espy, 1978).

I want to shift the focus, now, to the psychotherapeutic task of working with grief. Freud called professional attention to the necessity of the mourning labor; Perls offered the professional community some active methods for its facilitation. Building on Freud's observation, Perls recognized that loss without a grieving for that loss constitutes a situation of unfinished business. He then provided procedures for the completion of that process.

Basically, the Gestalt approach is to support grieving. This means, in any way needed, to facilitate the grieving process while frustrating any attempts to avoid it. (This includes the frustration of depression.) Gestalt is an active therapy, emphasizing organismic involvement.

To understand the reason for the Gestalt procedures requires a recognition of the components of grieving and of their relationships. Using the Contact/Withdrawal Model (Smith, 1979, 1985) I conceptualize the unit of grieving as follows:

Loss→Need to grieve→Organismic tension→Feeling sad→
Action of crying→Relief

This unit of grieving, or grief cycle, can vary in intensity, frequency, and number of repetitions, depending on the degree of loss. In each case, however, the loss calls for grieving and that organismic need leads to a state of organismic tension or arousal. That state of tension is subjectively experienced as the emotion of sadness. The organismic action called forth by that emotion is crying. When the crying is sufficient to match the need, for that particular unit of grieving, there is a sense of relief or satisfaction. Some time may then pass during which the need to grieve again builds up to the point of once again being experienced.

Since the grief cycle requires awareness of the loss, awareness of the need to grieve, awareness and allowing of the tension or bodily arousal to build, awareness of sadness, and the activity of crying, the incompleteness of any of these decreases the amount of relief which can be experienced. So, the therapeutic focus is on any inadequacy of *awareness, arousal,* or *crying activity.*

In his classic article, "Saying Goodby," Stephen Tobin (1971, 1975) has described the use of the empty-chair dialogue in the Gestalt procedure of saying good-bye to someone not literally present. In addition to his description of the method, he has provided an instructional clinical transcript re-creating some of this work. I want to elaborate on the basic method outlined by Tobin.

The Gestalt procedure of saying good-bye is the same regardless of what is being grieved—a person, an animal, an inanimate object, or an idea. The basic guideline is to create a situation in which the patient can psychodramatically encounter the object of loss. (For heuristic purposes I will talk about a person as the object of loss.) So, I invite the patient to imagine the person sitting in the empty chair. Depending on how experienced the patient is in doing empty-chair work, I may do some preliminary work to increase the vividness of the image of the person. This can include the suggestion of seeing the person as clearly as possible, hearing that person say "hello," and even smelling that person, if smell had been a strong memory of that person. (Sometimes there are vivid memories of an odor associated with a person, such as a pipe-tobacco smoke, a perfume, or such.) Bringing the person into the here-and-now experience of the patient is the first step of the psychodrama.

When the person is experienced with an adequate degree of vividness, I move to the second step. I ask the patient to sit for a few moments and just see what it is like to be with the person. I may suggest that the patient feel whatever emotions arise.

The third step is to invite the patient to tell the person whatever he or she is feeling. This is what is sometimes stated in Gestalt therapy as the "no gossiping rule" (Levitsky & Perls, 1970). The idea is to *talk to* the person rather than to *talk about* the person. (A little experimenting with this is sufficient to demonstrate that talking to someone is far more emotionally impactful than talking about the person.) I invite the patient to say all he or she is thinking and feeling, as long as the thoughts are not avoidances of the here-and-now experience. There are three elements which are important in this expression: *appreciations, resentments,* and *regrets.* I encourage the full expression of each of these, and call attention to any element which has not been expressed spontaneously. Appreciations reflect the good memories and good feelings, the love for the person. On the other hand, resentments represent the unpleasant memories and bad feelings for the person, in extreme form, one's hatred. Regrets are the acknowledgment of things not being or not having been as one would like. A good, clean grieving seems to require the expression of all three. Otherwise, some piece of unfinished business remains.

The fourth step is making this empty chair monologue into an empty chair dialogue. This is done by inviting the patient to switch chairs, "be" the person, and respond to what the patient has said. This shuttling back and forth allows for amplification of the feelings, and a sense of completion and satisfaction. The timing of these switches is part of the artistry of an adept Gestalt therapist.

These, then, are the four steps in the Gestalt procedure for saying good–bye. I attend to the grief cycle during this saying good–bye, watching for any *avoidance of full awareness, avoidance of allowing the buildup of arousal,* or *avoidance of crying.* The points of avoidance are the points for therapeutic intervention. Often, the intervention needs only to be a calling attention to, or an encouragement of what is being avoided. Some examples are as follows: "Will you look at him when you say that?" "Stay with what you're experiencing." "Feel what you're feeling." "Tell him you know he isn't coming back." Such interventions focus on awareness. Since arousal is quelled by inadequate breathing, the avoidance of arousal may be dealt with by interventions such as: "Don't hold your breath." "Keep breathing." In order to frustrate the avoidance of crying, the therapist could say: "Let that out." "Let your tears come." "Let the sound out." "Make sound."

When simply calling attention to an avoidance, or verbally encouraging the flow of the grief cycle is not a potent enough intervention, my bias is to intervene with body work. Such work may be aimed at increasing awareness, increasing breathing, and in turn, arousal, or at softening muscular tensions which are inhibiting crying. The rationale and techniques of such body interventions are presented in detail in *The Body in Psychotherapy* (Smith, 1985).

I want to close with a quote that I take as an expression of wisdom and of hope. Hemingway (1970, p. 296) put the following words into the mouth of Thomas Hudson:

> You always feel better and
> you always get over your
> remorse. There's only one
> thing you don't get over
> and that is death.

REFERENCES

Colgrove, M., Bloomfield, H., & McWilliams, P. (1976). *How to survive the loss of a love*. New York: Bantam.

Emerson, P., & Smith, E. (1974) Contributions of Gestalt psychology to Gestalt therapy. *The Counseling Psychologist,* 4(4), 8-12.

Espy, W. (1978) *Thou improper, thou uncommon noun*. New York: Clarkson N. Potter.

Freud, S. (1963). Mourning and Melancholia. In P. Rieff, (Ed.), *General psychological theory*. New York: Collier.

Hemingway, E. (1970). *Islands in the stream*. New York: Charles Scribner's Sons.

Levitsky, A., & Perls, F. (1970). The rules and games of Gestalt therapy. In J. Fagan, and I. Shepherd (Eds.) *Gestalt therapy now*. Palo Alto, CA: Science & Behavior Books.

Perls, F. (1947, 1969). *Ego, hunger, and aggression*. New York: Vintage.

Perls, F. (1969). *Gestalt therapy verbatim*. New York: Bantam.

Perls, F. (1975). *Legacy from Fritz*. Palo Alto, California: Science & Behavior Books.

Rycroft, C. (1968). *A critical dictionary of psychoanalysis*. New York: Basic Books.

Smith, E. (1979). Seven decision points. *Voices*. 15(3), 45-50.

Smith, E. (1985). *The body in psychotherapy*. Jefferson, NC: McFarland.

Sperling, S. (1981). *Tenderfeet and ladyfingers*. New York: Viking.

Tobin, S. (1971, 1975). Saying Goodbye. In J. Stevens (Ed.) *Gestalt is*. Moab, UT: Real People Press.

Shared Grief as an Impetus
for Psychotherapy

Herbert M. Potash

ABSTRACT. The unexpected death of a long-term psychotherapy patient brought the therapist and husband together in an intensive grief sharing meeting. This encounter established the foundation for the husband's subsequent personal therapy. The husband's positive reaction to his wife's prior psychotherapy, coupled with the shared grief, facilitated and expedited his recovery from her death and his effective participation in personal psychotherapy.

Traditional training in psychotherapy demands a rigid demarcation between individual psychotherapy and work with families and couples. Although we continually address the needs of both members of a marriage in marital therapy, it is rare for us to have any contact with the spouse of a patient we are seeing in individual psychotherapy. Not only would such contact break the traditional psychotherapy rules, but it would also become fraught with such transference and countertransference issues so as usually to be unproductive and at times even to be ethically questionable.

One set of circumstances which nonetheless questions the advisability of noncontact with our patients' spouses surrounds emergency situations. Psychological and medical emergencies can and will necessitate that we either initiate or respond to such contact, and the type of emergency will often determine both the length and the intensity of this dialogue. Being aware of the potential danger of such contact with our patients' families may, at times, enable us to monitor the contact quite effectively. It may also lead us to break those rules when unique circumstances warrant it, as evidenced in the following clinical situation.

I had been working with Kathleen, a 50-year-old married woman, in weekly individual psychotherapy over a 2-year period. She arrived at one crucial psychotherapy session having just been informed by her physician that her radiologist had confirmed the presence of a small and operable

Herbert M. Potash is a professor and the Co-Director of Clinical Training at the Madison campus of Fairleigh Dickinson University. He has a part-time private practice of psychotherapy and is the author of *Inside Clinical Psychology: A Handbook for Graduate Students and Interns,* Fairleigh Dickinson University, Madison, NJ 07940.

brain tumor. This possibility had been raised four and a half years earlier when Kathleen suffered a total hearing loss in one ear. The physician requested that she consult with a neurologist to evaluate the possibility of surgery.

Kathleen understandably was very afraid and depressed, and I remember trying to provide her with strength and encouragement. This particular symptomatology of neurologically based hearing loss was all too familiar to me, as a close relative had died as a result of such a tumor. I decided in that session that we must take quick and effective action to ensure that Kathleen be given the best possible medical care. Accordingly, I referred her to the chief of service at a world-famous facility for neurological disorders. Kathleen, though still quite frightened, appeared also to be reassured; and in a few weeks she was able both to have and to report upon her neurological consultation.

The news she brought was very encouraging. An operation was recommended, but it was a relatively minor form of brain surgery with an excellent prognosis. The neurologist expected no long-range negative effects; fatalities occurred in only 1-2% of such surgical cases. Kathleen was so encouraged that she arranged to have the surgery performed as soon as possible. It was scheduled for a few weeks hence which, in fact, coincided with the second day of my summer vacation.

When I later called the hospital for a report on Kathleen's condition, I was informed there was no significant change: She was "still critical." Massive post-surgical complications had produced brain swelling, and Kathleen's prognosis was very poor. Feeling stunned, I gave the hospital my phone number in case the family wanted to speak with me, although I did not consider that a likely possibility. However, my patient's husband, Michael, did phone shortly thereafter to inform me of what had occurred. He called the next day to report no change in his wife's condition, and no hope for recovery was offered. Michael called the third day to tell me of his wife's death and the subsequent funeral arrangement.

While I usually have no personal contact with family members of my individual psychotherapy cases, I had made somewhat of an exception with Kathleen's family. I had given Kathleen the name of a psychotherapist as a referral for her adult daughter. I also had agreed to meet with her son when he was visiting the family from his distant home. This meeting was a productive one, and in fact I met with the son 6 months afterwards when he was again visiting with his family. I had no contact with the husband nor any other contact with the family until I received those phone calls about Kathleen's condition.

Having worked with Kathleen for 2 years, I was deeply shaken and upset over her tragic surgery and death. The professional in me of course recognized that Michael's grief was necessarily far deeper than my own, so I tried to be as supportive as I could in those very awkward telephone conversations. It seemed odd to find Michael turning to me for advice and support, especially since I was a stranger to him. At this very trying time, undoubtedly the last thing I anticipated was a call for support, particularly since I had instigated the arrangements for this death-producing surgery.

I still had not personally met Michael; and as I had only met the son twice, I decided not to return for Kathleen's funeral. It was a difficult decision and a distressing time, especially because Kathleen was the first and only patient of mine to have died.

Upon my return home there was a taped phone message from Michael requesting an appointment for psychotherapy. I was not then prepared to see Michael as a psychotherapy patient. I was still working through my own grief and misplaced guilt; I did not believe that I could readily change my allegiance nor was I sure I would be able to view Michael in an impartial and objective light. Still, I felt an obligation to at least meet with him and personally express my condolences. Therefore I set up an appointment for the following morning.

That initial meeting lasted over 2 hours. It was certainly not a traditional psychotherapy session. We, in fact, mourned together. Michael needed to tell me that he was very grateful for my assistance to Kathleen, which had made the last 2 years of their marriage very rewarding to them both. Michael apparently needed to experience concretely a personal connection with me and to be able to enter into and to share in this unknown and private sphere of his wife's life.

Even more important, Michael himself was feeling lost and overwhelmed by Kathleen's death. In many ways he had been leaning on his wife during their 30 years of marriage. And at some level Michael was hoping that I would assume his wife's long-standing role and provide him with direction and answers. He acknowledged that he was not able to resume work, even though he knew it was time to do so. Michael was feeling so desperate that he requested we begin regular individual psychotherapy.

It was very important to point out to Michael that his need to grieve was his most immediate and overwhelming need. Being extremely depressed because his wife had suddenly died was very natural. These feelings of grief are distinct from the usual range of needs that are serviced in psychotherapy. Accordingly, I told Michael that he was experiencing natural, painful responses to his wife's death. I stated that he would certainly remain in deep pain for a period of time because he had been very close to his wife. Still, Michael had to resume his work and life chores.

I told Michael I would consider immediate personal therapy with him only if he was unable to resume work. Otherwise, we could meet after some time had elapsed, provided that Michael found it too difficult to put his life in order by himself. Certainly, I said, we would not meet regularly for at least a month. Also, while I nodded assent to his request that I send him a bill, I knew I could not charge him for this meeting. Too much of my own need to share my grief had been expressed at that session. There was no way I could charge for such services.

Recalling Kathleen's psychotherapy, I was aware that Michael himself had significant personal problems and had been routinely resisting her repeated suggestions that he enter therapy. If he was now to begin effective personal psychotherapy, it must be because he himself felt a commitment to personal change and not because of his more immediate and overwhelming personal loss.

Not long after this suggested one-month period I received a call from Michael's daughter, who expressed much concern over her father's depression. I told her that I would be willing to meet with him if he personally called me, which he did. Subsequently, we began a regular course of weekly individual psychotherapy sessions which are now entering their fifth month.

I now know that because of my psychotherapeutic work with Kathleen, I was initially held in high positive regard by Michael. This connection was significantly increased by our shared loss and mutual grief over her death. The first meeting with Michael shortly after Kathleen's death became the basis of a connection that then was capable of extension into the wider bounds of individual psychotherapy.

Because I had been Kathleen's therapist and trusted confidant, now that I am Michael's therapist I can most legitimately give him permission to build a new life for himself. This is currently one of the primary roles that I assume with Michael. There are, however, concomitant problems that were created by my having functioned as Kathleen's therapist prior to my work with Michael.

In this particular case I am accorded too much expertise by Michael. While this in part may be due to his own personality dynamics, it is also due to Kathleen's positive therapeutic experience. Consequently, it is nececessary to repeatedly deflect the sense of power back to Michael where it belongs. As the psychotherapist in such a case, I have discovered a more difficult dynamic that I can deal with only outside the therapy session. At times I find that my expectations of Michael are simply extensions of Kathleen's perceptions rather than my own independent and objective assessment of his strengths and weaknesses. Whenever Michael's behavior is at odds with those expectations, I can see the subtle historical influence at work and regroup. After a few months of work I can now much more clearly recognize Michael for himself, unclouded by Kathleen. Still, this serves as a reminder that patients' perceptions of the significant others in their lives can be tinged by personal need.

The dimension of our therapeutic work that surrounds the complicated transferential issues is usually not discussed. Michael is working very hard to change behavior patterns that Kathleen had long criticized and which he had typically ignored. Michael's high motivation for behavioral change may very well represent a symbolic repaying of a debt he has to her. If such is the underlying case, he will not profit from its discussion. As Michael's psychotherapist I recognize that he is working to attain better mental health, and the source of his motivation becomes unimportant.

At times traumatic circumstances, such as death, demand that we dispute and even recast long-standing rules for professional behavior. While Michael could indeed have recuperated if he had consulted other therapists, he chose not to contact another prior therapist whom he respected. How he felt at that particular time dictated his need to work with me. Even though this meant facing many potentially difficult transference and countertransference issues, it seemed a better risk rather than attempting a referral where Michael's likelihood of follow-through was questionable. In this situation I was endowed with a high degree of therapeutic power which could significantly ease Michael's mourning, and I therefore chose to use it.

In such a case it was necessary to transfer my allegiance to Michael, after Kathleen had died, in order to help Michael rebuild his life. I made the difficult decision of choosing to help Michael work through his grief rather than following traditional therapeutic rules. This has proved to be correct insofar that it is working, but it is a choice I hope never to have to make again. This experience nonetheless demonstrates that our prior therapeutic work with a spouse can be used advantageously to help a patient overcome his or her grief.

Children of Alcoholics:
The Subterranean Grieving Process

Jefferson Breen

ABSTRACT. Repressed dimensions of grieving as they relate to the off-spring of alcoholics are discussed from a clinician's point of view. The author draws liberally on the model of normal grieving as put forth by Dr. Elisabeth Kübler-Ross.

Approximately 25 to 28 million children and adults in the United States grew up, or are presently living, in alcoholic homes (Ackerman, 1983, p.4). Recent research points to the likelihood that the child of an alcoholic is four times more likely to become an alcoholic than the child from a nonalcoholic family (Black & Bucky, 1984).

From a psychological perspective, children of alcoholics are confronted by a devastating reality. Their emotions are repressed and altered, not shared, and when communicating they usually do so in a vindictive, ex-ternalized, blaming, and nonresponsible manner. While the usual barom-eter of a harmonious and healthy family is consistency and predictability, the child in an alcoholic family lives constantly with inconsistency and un-predictability. The "normal" child in a "healthy" family has the oppor-tunity to share feelings, give and receive attention, live within an open clearly defined system, become autonomous, and live within a combina-tion of roles that will usually lead developmentally to becoming a healthy person. The child of an alcoholic becomes "stuck" in a role that enables him or her to survive at best, and ultimately develops into a role that even-tually fails in the attempt to become a healthy adult.

During the past 5 years I have become increasingly more sensitized as a psychotherapist to the particular psychological problems of children of alcoholics.

One of the major themes that I perceive within this client's system is the "bottled-up" (pun intended!) grief that he or she carries within into adulthood as a result of the alcoholic parent being "absent" and the co-dependdent spouse's preoccupation with the alcholic.

Jefferson Breen, Ed.D. is a licensed Psychologist who has been in practice as a psychotherapist for 20 years. In addition, he is an Associate Professor of Psychology at Fitchburg (Mass.) State Col-lege. 262 Boston Turnpike, P.O. Box 65, Turnpike Station, Shrewsbury, MA 01545.

Black (1981, p. 77) points out that the child of an alcoholic experiences a grieving process similar to the process other people feel when they lose someone close through death or are facing an impending loss. However, the crucial difference between the two is that the child of an alcoholic is confronted with an "altered" grief that is repressed for an alcoholic parent who is psychologically "dead" or "absent" yet is physically alive. As I indicated in the title of this paper, the word "subterranean" will be used for the child, adolescent, or adult member of an alcoholic family system. Although the grief may not manifest itself on the surface, it still festers within.

Black further notes the parallel stages that the child of an alcoholic or "lost child" and the normal individual experience as they journey through their grief similar to the Kübler-Ross (1975) model. The first stage, denial, may serve the healthy as well as lost child's objective of numbing self from the chilling reality of dealing with a loss. However, the healthy person usually moves from this discrediting stage to the next, anger, whereas the child of an alcoholic may remain fixated perpetually in this stage. My clinical experience has noted, in particular, that children of alcoholics may readily admit that a spouse is an alcoholic but will continually deny, or not accept, the severe emotional consequences they suffer as a result of this loss.

The next stage, anger, is also marked by experiential differences for the healthy person dealing with loss and the lost child. Typically, the healthy person expresses anger outwardly in a variety of ways and often with at least one significant other. "How can you be doing this (leaving) to me?" "I won't let this happen!" "I hate you for doing this to me!" The child of an alcoholic does express anger, but is typically much less overt than the healthy person. In reality, he or she is frequently covert particularly in the respect that he or she internalizes his anger and frequently carries it in this twisted sense through life. I have seen the anger of the lost child express itself more frequently in the garb of guilt. "Maybe if I had not talked back to Dad . . . or had done better in school . . . or had made the school basketball team, Dad would not have been drunk at Mom's birthday party."

The next stage, bargaining, is often witnessed in the mode of spiritual or religious expression. The healthy person will pray for a reprieve from loss and grief by requesting that the loved one who is dying be granted health. Usually, the grim reality is accepted in time that this repreive is not possible. The religious perspective of the healthy person usually provides parameters for the ultimate acceptance of this loss, and this aspect of grief is resolved and incorporated positively into the spiritual system. However, the child of an alcoholic usually has a different response. A form of grandiosity oftentimes emerges. "If I say my prayers more faithfully . . . or go to church more regularly . . . or read the Bible more often, Dad will stop or lessen his drinking.'' Sadly enough, I would wager that adult children of alcoholics suffer a form of spiritual depletion more frequently than the grieving person who lives in a nonalcoholic environment. This phenomenon occurs because this adult child usually experiences all of the incantations as unheard. If anything, this spiritual imploring witnesses an even greater loss in that the alcoholic family member deteriorates even further. Tragically, the alcoholic parent, unlike someone who is dying from a disease other than alcoholism, lingers seemingly interminably in the life of the lost child. He or she remains a tragic testimony to the child that prayer does not work. In the perceptual phenomena of the lost child, it may even seem to worsen it.

The fourth stage in the Kübler-Ross paradigm is depression. Although the normal individual and the child of an alcoholic both experience the lack of power and helplessness that accompany their loss, the lost child usually has a seemingly infinite reminder of this diminution of their healthy control. Mother and/or father, unless treatment intervention occurs, remain often as perpetual reminders of the powerlessness that their offspring holds in rendering their alcoholism ineffective. In short, the individual from the functional family system sees a concrete termination to loss usually within a fairly predictable time sequence. The child of an alcoholic must endure the endless uncertainty of the alcoholic parent's continued disease. From a clinical perspective, the depression that accompanies this grim realization usually spills over to many of the lost child's later relationships, including marriage.

The final stage, acceptance, is one that is markedly different for the child of an alcoholic and the person from the healthy family system. The normal person may well experience temporal difficulty in the acceptance of the loss of the loved one. The literature is certainly filled with examples of the interminable grief that some individuals endure. However, upon a more careful examination of the background of these individuals, we discover that although they may not come from within an alcoholic family system, they usually do come from a dysfunctional system of some sort. In short, their psychodynamics are such that they have difficulty in "letting go." However, the usual step for the healthy individual in the final stage of the Kübler-Ross paradigm is acceptance of the loss and, ultimately, getting on with one's own life.

The child of an alcoholic, in certain respects, begins a passive form of nonacceptance very early in the grieving process. My experience has revealed that this lost child, probably at an unconscious level, realizes that his or her battle to impede the steady deterioration of the alcoholic parent is hopeless. Yet as in all the previous stages of grief, there is always the corporal reminder of possible remission. However, the final result for the child of an alcoholic, unless there is an actual early physical termination in the alcoholic parent's life, is more of an *admission* that the alcoholic parent is psychologically and spiritually lost, but a passive nonacceptance, because of the physical presence of the parent, that the loss can somehow be repealed.

I would like to share several of my clinical experiences with adult children of alcoholics, in particular, who exemplify various stages of "arrest" in the Kübler-Ross sequential model of grieving. The first stage, denial, as I mentioned earlier, is a complex one. For many children of alcoholics, there is no passage beyond this stage.

Brighton M. was a 40-year-old professional administrator who entered psychotherapy several years after his first marriage failed. Although several important themes emerged during Brighton's intermittent therapy, (for example, authority issues in his work as well as stress-related problems both at home and at his job), Brighton danced around the issue of alcoholism. Although he shared the fact that his mother was an alcoholic who eventually died from cirrhosis of the liver, and that his father more than likely died from alcoholism, he evaded discussion of any possible connection that he might have with the disease. After several years of his spastic involvement in psychotherapy, Brighton agreed to explore the possibility of his own alcoholism with the alcoholism counselor on my staff. In spite of the fact that this meeting was initiated by Brighton, it was clear to me that he was more interested in "going through the motions" as a type of token gesture to placate me, his primary psychotherapist. The upshot of the session between Brighton and my staff alcoholism counselor was an admission that he was an alcoholic. However, the therapy hit a roadblock, as it consistently did in the 3-year course of psychotherapy, when Brighton steadfastly admitted that "I am an alcoholic but I do not have a problem."

Although Brighton is typical of the adult child of an alcoholic in his denial, the emotive aspect of his therapy, namely his grieving for both his alcoholic parents may never be faced. For Brighton to acknowledge the full range of his alcoholism, it would be necessary to look not only at the physical loss of both parents, since Brighton was 13 when his father died and 19 when his mother died, but more significantly at the emotional loss of both parents long before their physical termination. In short, Brighton's deeply repressed grieving that was abetted by his alcoholism and manifested itself in a masqueraded depression, was safe, at least, as long as it could remain safely nestled in the cocoon of denial.

Anger is the next stage in the grieving process that the adult child of the alcoholic invariably becomes ensnared in. Although denial may or may not be successfully resolved in the sense that the adult child of an alcoholic has either admitted and accepted the fact of his or her alcoholism or denied it, anger, or its denial, is another manifestation of developmental arrest for many adult children of alcoholics.

One of the major manifestations of anger can be seen within the pattern of what I have come to call "mistargeted" anger within the adult child of the alcoholic. Joe L., an extremely successful professional, an alcoholic, and one of six adult children of an alcoholic parent, obviously came from a severely dysfunctional family system. Joe's father, a prominent professional, was the patriarch of the family, and he communicated his need for power and approval to his children daily. For example, Joe related his father's insistence that he be addressed as "Dr." during the children's formative years; how he physically abused the children when they "misbehaved," and kept his own alcoholism secretly "stuffed" in the closet. The relationship between Joe's father and mother was obviously one that was cool and distant. Joe related that his mother experienced a "nervous breakdown" when he was approximately 18 months old and that he was separated from her for about 6 months while she was hospitalized.

Joe was an angry person. He maintained a group of friends who remained loyal to him despite the antagonistic stance he frequently took toward them. Joe, nevertheless, was a difficult person to relate to. In a fundamental respect, Joe expected an incredible amount of loyalty in his relationships, and expressed his wrath and anger vehemently when these expectations were not met. Psychodynamically, Joe constantly projected the loss of his parents onto his friends, lovers, and even his professional associates in an effort to gain surrogates for his "lost" parents. Interestingly, Joe identified with his father, in spite of occasional outbursts of anger toward him, through the use of intimidation in relationships, his own alcoholism, and by following in his father's footsteps professionally. However, the significant point to observe within the context of this article is that Joe's fixation of anger removed him from having to deal with the massive grief he experienced in the loss of his parents as human beings early in his life. Joe particularly referred to the feelings of sadness that were deeply imbedded in him but that he could not ignite because of his inability to cry. This blockage for Joe is one of the major difficulties that adult children of alcoholics experience and on which I shall comment more fully later in this article.

Bargaining, as I mentioned earlier, is a stage in the grieving process that manifests itself frequently via a spiritual void insofar as the adult child of the alcoholic is concerned. One of the cues that frequently leads me to consider the question of how deeply alcoholism affected the adult child is the degree of resentment expressed toward religion. George C. was an educator who was quite competent and respected professionally. During the early stages of therapy, George made periodic casual references to the folly of religion. Since these remarks were infrequent and stated in the voice of an academician, I did not pay particular note to them. Although the central theme of George's therapy was his recent divorce, I decided to explore, with his permission, some of George's earlier history. Although George was quite amenable to respond to my question of whether there was alcoholism in his family, he was subtly evasive in terms of continuing the exploration of alcoholism and the effect it had on him. There was a marked lack of affect, in particular, as George talked matter-of-factly about his father's alcoholism for most of his childhood and all of his adolescence. George was also in an entrenched position of defense toward his mother who was the co-dependent spouse in this systemic dysfunctioning. In other words, George's mother was his sole source of nurturance and support during his formative years and George was especially reluctant to move into that territory in a meaningful way despite the fact that he would talk about several of the limitations in his relationship with his mother.

During one particular session, I inquired of George what his religious background was. He stated that he had been born into Catholicism but he recalled that he had left it as early as age 11. George recalled this fact with a sense of accomplishment. As I explored this break with him, he said that he simply could not accept the principles or historical base of Catholicism, especially the way the nuns, who were his teachers, taught it. As a therapist, it would have been easy to have left the issue of religion at that point unless George were to resume it again. However, my clinical intuition urged me to probe a bit more since George seemed receptive enough to continue.

As George continued his verbal ruminations regarding his early religious involvement, he recalled how his seventh-grade teacher inquired of the class periodically as to whether they had said their prayers the evening before. George recalled the anger and resentment he felt about this intrusion as well as the guilt he experienced as a result of the lie he felt "forced" to commit. I asked him to close his eyes for a moment and imagine what he would have liked to have said if he could have. There was a lengthy silence as George sat there with his eyes closed. Somehow I could feel that something very powerful had been stirred in George and that it was about to emerge. George's body began to tremble and a small trickle of tears began to stream from his eyes. "I can recall praying desperately night after night to God begging that he would have my father stop drinking. I promised that I would never do anything wrong again." George began to chuckle through his tears as he said this since, upon reflection, he remembered that he was the near-perfect child. However, given the dysfunctional relationship pattern that placed him squarely in the middle of his mother and father, he could never do enough. The more he came close to pleasing his mother, which made his alliance stronger with her, the more he, in turn, distanced himself from his father.

George continued his vignette about the meaning of prayer for him. "How often after I had prayed desperately to God would I hear my father come in "smashed." After years of prayer, I decided that God did not want to hear my prayers. So my answer to your question about what I really wanted to say to the nun who asked whether we said our prayers the night before was, "No, I did not say my prayers. Why should I? I'm not sure that there is a God anyway. He never listened to my prayers."

Depression, of all the clinical manifestations, is perhaps the most frequent expression of the arrested state of grief that the child of an alcoholic wallows in. Alcoholism itself is one of the ways that the lost child attempts to combat this depression. And, as stated earlier in a statistical sense, it may well be the central dynamic behind the adult child of an alcoholic being four times more likely to become an alcoholic himself.

My clinical experience would perhaps be epitomized best by Florence C., a 34-year-old woman whose primary reason for entering therapy was her consistent inability to complete tasks, to maintain relationships of any kind and, in short, to give up consistently in virtually almost any endeavor she undertook. She described the acute depression she experienced most of her life, but was now deeply concerned over the chronic depression she had been immersed in for several years now.

Florence eventually related the fact of her mother's "closet" alcoholism and how she had struggled for years to steer her mother away from this "horror." However, as would be predicted, all of Florence's efforts were for naught. As a result, Florence developed an attitude of hopelessness and helplessness that manifested itself in depression. Florence's simple statement, "What's the use of trying?" captured the central dynamics of frustration and despair that she injected into virtually all of her life situations. In short, she assumed failure to be the concomitant of any endeavor she attempted, given the prototype of her relationship with her mother.

The final stage, that of desperation and despair, is one that could be exemplified by the previous illustration of George C.'s later therapy. Although George made several significant strides toward becoming a healthier, happier human being, he stated in his final session: "Although I can accept my father's alcoholism and live more comfortably within myself, I still look at him when we visit, and feel twinges of remorse in my soul. I know now that I'll never fully accept the tragedy of this living death." Since adult children of alcoholics tend to position themselves similarly in this stage of grieving, suffice it to say that there is a universal sentiment of feeling alone and that no one else could relate to their suffering. Further, there is a stance of resoluteness since they perceive that there never can be a final solution to their situation. In short, their grieving is marked by a quiet desperation and depression.

The significance of all these stages of grief that children of alcoholics pass through is that, unlike the "normal" child, many children of alcoholics are unable to communicate their feelings of grief. The anger, fear, guilt, and tears are stored deep within them since the role models they have within their family system validate the non- or inappropriate expression of these feelings. Therefore, as in the case of normal children who can deal with crises in their lives through the natural release of their feelings, children of alcoholics repress the natural flow or release of their affect. In a significant and tragic sense, the child of the alcoholic may journey through his or her entire life in a state of subterranean grief.

In order to be more specific, I shall now explore the specific emotions that the adult child represses in particular. In a normal functioning family, the major release for the grieving individual(s) is crying. We need no more than to observe this phenomenon across virtually all cultures as a universal means of expressing one's feelings about the personal loss that one has incurred. In short, crying is the biological release or, as Keleman (1981) has pointed out, the body speaking its mind. Although crying is difficult for some people because of several factors, children of alcoholics deal with their tears in two fundamentally unique ways. First, they learn that they should not cry; and second, they cry alone, and oftentimes in very morose ways.

One of the basic cues that will lead me to inquire whether a client may have "survived" in an alcoholic home is the incredible block that impedes the flow of tears. Often in an early session, a client will relate a particular occurrence or event to me that has overt tragic implications for him or her. However, a rather blank, hollow, and expressionless countenance usually conceals the tragedy within. Although I may choose to note this rather contradictory fact to the client, it is usually received in a passive or computerized fashion. Nancy M. reminded me, approximately eight sessions after I had mirrored back her lack of affect when she described how her younger teenaged brother had been killed in Vietnam, that she had carried this reflection of mine within her and needed to talk about it. She recalled how the norm that evolved in her family was one of "no tears" regardless of the precipitant. She went on to explain that her codependent mother never cried despite the fact that virtually "every day of her childhood contained at least one event that could necessitate tears." She went on to share with me that her mother was her only hope in the face of her father's alcoholism and that she modeled herself after her. She recalled further that her younger brothers were given specific messages by her mother that added up to the fact that "boys shouldn't cry."

Nancy further illustrated the second dimension of crying several months into her therapy. The depression that she had now given in to was overt during our sessions. She had opened up to the loss of her childhood and her tears were on the threshold of letting go. For several sessions, Nancy's grief would express itself best literally by an occasional tear or two slowly rolling down her cheek. Although I would note this and attempt to provide her with reassurance, namely that it was healthy and "OK" to cry, Nancy would usually put the brakes on her tears.

However, during a particular session in which I had reflected back to Nancy how her feeling that the relationship with her spouse was so one-sided, sounded so analogous to her relationship with her parents, she stated: "Yes, I feel as if I do most of the giving in almost every relationship that I'm in. Even as I recall my relationship with my parents, it was always a matter of my attempt to please them so that they would not fight—or that one or the other of them would not be depressed, I could not afford the time simply to be a kid." At that point, Nancy stopped talking. For several moments, a small stream of tears rolled gently down her cheeks. Her eyes reached the point of saturation, serving as an overflowing pool that was attempting to stretch beyond its limits to contain her tears. Her entire body began to tremble gently as if some incredible energy was screaming to become unleashed. Then a sob that I could best describe as a sound that seemed as if it had been muffled with several layers of insulation emerged. It was the sound of a lost child whose faint cry echoed almost unheard from deep within a heavily wooded forest. Nancy struggled both within and without to get in touch with and, at the same time, to cover over the sobs. For several minutes, the struggle ensued with my gentle encouragement but it slowly ebbed away. Nancy sat motionless as the session came closer to ending and stated: "Maybe I can still find that little girl."

The importance of this account of Nancy is to point out her tremendous ordeal in the natural release of tears. Grieving in the form of tears for the adult child of the alcoholic is an emotion that remains subterranean, yet seething within, and in some cases, perpetually entombed.

Another of the repressed dimensions of grieving for the adult child is fear. Once again, in the normal state, the person facing a loss is usually free to express the fear being experienced. However, the child of the alcoholic usually lives in an environment that stimulates him or her to be chronically fearful. My clinical experience has taught me that the loss most feared by the child of the alcoholic is self–esteem or, as I like to describe it, personal worth. Children of alcoholics often would like to express the fear that they have of being confronted by an alcoholic parent who is on a binge. Often the fear is one of embarrassment that they would have to deal with as a result of their alcoholic parent humiliating them in the presence of their peers or siblings. The important point to be emphasized here is that the incredibly powerful emotion of fear, which needs an appropriate outlet to express itself, remains subterranean within the phenomenological world of the child of an alcoholic. One more painful dimension is added to the hidden grieving process of the lost child. And as in the case of any repressed emotion, the strength of this feeling, turned inward, becomes only that much more powerful as a potential psychological slayer of the child of an alcoholic.

Robert B.'s father was an alcoholic. As an adult in therapy with me,

Robert almost always came across as a "nice" person. He apologized incessantly whenever he was late for a session and usually let me know when the session time was concluded. I sensed the anger that he kept hidden so well yet I did not find any openings to pursue this invisible emotion until approximately our eighth session. When I inquired of Robert if he could ever recall being angry, he pondered the question for several moments. Then, in a rather mechanical fashion, he recalled an incident when he was 18 years old that involved his first girlfriend and his parents. Quite simply, Robert's alcoholic father had "stumbled" into Robert's girlfriend's father's business, and drunkenly insisted on being given a job because he was unemployed. When Robert came home from high school basketball practice later that day, what had transpired earlier that day "came out in the wash" eventually from his mother. Robert recalled the pained emptiness that ran through him and then, as he described it, the sudden impulse to beat his father to death. As Robert related the story, he then proceeded to attempt that very thing and had to be forcibly pulled off his father by his mother and cousin. What this lost child demonstrated was how an expression of feeling that is chronically denied can be explosive and frequently unpredictable in its occasional appearance. However, once again, another powerful emotion, namely anger, which is such a vital part of the grieving process, is contained within and, if and when expressed, may literally be excessive, inappropriate, and oftentimes explosive.

As I have observed the healthy development of my 18-month-old daughter, I have marveled at the normal expression of her anger, fear, and tears. It is comforting to see the *in vivo* expression of these natural emotions. We all have the inner capacity to communicate them, yet, all too tragically, the child of the alcoholic learns not to. For that child, the normal ebb and flow of life, so often experienced healthily through the process of grieving, becomes a conditioned nonresponse. Hopefully, in our future endeavors as psychotherapists, we shall be sensitized to this critical blockage or fixation.

REFERENCES

Ackerman, R. (1983). *Children of alcoholics* (2nd ed.). Holmes Beach, FL: Learning Publication.

Black, C. (1981). *It will never happen to me.* Denver, CO: M.A.C. (Printing and Publications Division).

Black, C. & Bucky, W. (1984). Unpublished Research Report. San Diego, CA: Mission Bay Hospital.

Keleman, S. (1981). *Your body speaks its mind.* Berkeley, CA: Center Press.

Kubler-Ross, E. (1969). *On death and dying.* New York: MacMillan.

Men and Grieving

E. Jean Scully

ABSTRACT. Counseling skills with men in grief after the deaths of their children. The author's experience in grief counseling spans a 10-year period.

My intention in raising the many issues involved with men and grieving is to alert and sensitize practitioners and the lay community to the unique and special needs of grieving men. It is my hope that together we can create an environment which encourages men to be more comfortable with their emotions; a society responsive to the needs of that half of the population whose feelings far exceed the limits they are permitted to express.

In my experience in counseling the bereaved, I have encountered many events which exemplify the emotional turbulence fathers experience after the death of their child. One father shared with me his pain as he tried to restore his infant's breathing. Another told of his uncontrollable rage and anger as he heard via the telephone that his child was in an automobile accident and was pronounced dead on arrival at a local hospital. Still another father was unable to speak of his agony as he watched the police race away with his baby daughter—telling him they were sure she was dead.

After the death of his 3-month-old-baby, John told me that he was in a state of solitude and that the cruel shock of the moment will never be completely erased from his mind. Flashbacks of that time are sporadic, independent thoughts, rather than an interwoven story of anguish and despair. There was no logic for him in this cruel event.

The night Michael attended the Bereavement Group meeting, the other grieving parents understood, identified, and consoled him as he told his story. Michael's 3-month-old-son, Keith, had died several weeks before of SIDS (Sudden Infant Death Syndrome)—a silent, cruel killer of babies that stalks the nursery and strikes without warning or predictability. While Michael drove to work that fateful morning, he turned the volume

E. Jean Scully is Director of Eastern New York Sudden Infant Death Syndrome (SIDS) Center. She is professor at the School of Social Welfare, State University of New York at Stony Brook, New York, and is also in the private practice of psychotherapy. 5 Starfire Drive, Centereach, NY 11720.

95

low on his 2-way radio and failed to hear the emergency call from his office. When he arrived at the office he was told to go to the hospital and meet his wife.

As Michael raced to the hospital his mind searched for an answer to who was in trouble. He was convinced his father had suffered a heart attack. As he entered the hospital lobby, a crying relative greeted him with the pallor that frequently colors the face of a bearer of bad tidings. Then he saw his wife. "Why was she crying and curling Keith's blanket in her arms?" Her eyes gave away the dreadful truth; Baby Keith was dead! Michael stood in shock, anger mounting in his chest as he tried to understand. "What happened?" "Why did this terrible thing occur?" "Did everyone do everything they could?"

As the day progressed, Michael took charge: informing other family members, arranging for the funeral, writing Keith's obituary, and making endless calls to spread the terrible story.

It wasn't until late that night when he was alone that Michael reviewed the day. He remembered that when he awoke that morning he had heard Keith gurgling in his crib; the sound echoed in Michael's memory. Why hadn't he gone in to see Keith this morning? "If only" he had held him one last time. "If only" he had checked the baby, maybe he would have sensed something. "If only" the volume was up on his 2-way radio, perhaps he might have saved Keith.

Stoically, Michael supported his wife and other children through the wake and funeral. He was conditioned to be strong, and to take care of others. When the funeral director needed information, it was Michael who was expected to provide the answers. When distant relatives and co-workers arrived, Michael was the one who provided consolation and explanations. It was he who listened to their well-meant platitudes, "So sorry" and "Can we do anything?" Michael answered in his head, "No, damn it—you can't do anything, you can't give me back my baby!! Doesn't anyone know how much I hurt inside?" Michael felt that a part of himself had been buried with his son. In the solitude of his car he reviewed his memories of Keith. He noticed a stain on the dashboard from the milk that had dripped some time ago from Keith's bottle. Michael vowed never to remove the stain, and never to hurt like this again. He constructed a wall to fence in his emotions, a wall made of sawdust. Protection at any price.

When a man's child dies, the emotional pain is overwhelming. His identity as protector and provider is shattered. Often the father is expected to assume the dreadful responsibilities of making funeral arrangements, identifying the precious body of his offspring, and consoling his devastated mate. He must undertake the task of informing his other children and grandparents of the death. All of this is expected of him without allowing him the opportunity to grieve openly.

Fathers must also deal with the "well-meaners": friends and relatives who ask how his wife/mate is "taking it," while forgetting to acknowledge the pain he is experiencing. These same people may remind him that he is young and can have another child, as if a replacement child is all that is needed to ease his excruciating agony. He will invariably be admonished: "Think of your other children." "Your wife will really need you now." "You must be strong for them."

Each year in this country thousands of pregnancies end in miscarriages, still-births, and neonatal deaths. Eight thousand infants die annually from Sudden Infant Death Syndrome and five thousand teenagers die from alcohol-related accidents. In 1980, in the United States there were 400,000 deaths of people under the age of 25.

The death of a child is contrary to the natural order of things. Life is to be passed on to children. Children are supposed to carry on their family name, to outlive their parents, and to perpetuate their parent's dreams.

My work with grieving fathers spans more than 10 years, and during that time I have learned from them. I have had to confront the prejudices I once held. Prejudices such as, "men don't feel as much as women" and "fathers aren't as close to children as mothers."

Studies have shown the male begins the bonding process to his unborn child as early as the last trimester of pregnancy. During these months males begin to dream and plan for their role as father. They have hopes and exciting ideas of the things they will do with their child. Many men share in the birth of their child, documenting the event with pictures, video tapes, and with plans to savor that moment forever.

A father whose 11-year-old son was run over by a truck shared the "if only's" running through his mind. "If only" he hadn't let Bobby cross the street alone. "If only" he had forbidden Bobby to go to that store. "If only" he had kissed him goodbye that morning. "If only" he had played ball the night before. "If only" this could be a nightmare and not be real.

Thoughts like these plague the grieving person's mind for a long time. They ponder hundreds of "if only's" and "I should have/could have's." This is a natural part of the denial stage of the grieving process.

Severe grief reactions such as extreme anger, guilt, and depression may be exhibited by a father who has been predeceased by his child. The despair he experiences over the loss of the child and the loss of part of himself can be overwhelming. The child is the father's conduit to the past as well as the bridge to the future. The child carries on family tradition and a sense of immortality that fathers invest in emotionally. When his child dies, a father's dreams are lost and shattered. No longer can he fantasize about the daughter who would have become the ballerina, the mother, director, doctor; or the son who might have been the president, banker, chief, father.

Fathers feel impotent as they try to breathe life into the limp, lifeless bodies of their babies; as they race to emergency rooms begging, screaming, crying out their anguish, hoping the medical world can stop the death. Many have resorted to alcohol, drugs, silence, and stoic behavior to dull this inconceivable distortion of reality. A father is expected to provide financial, emotional, intellectual, and moral support for his group. When he is not able to save his child, he questions the very essence of his ability to insure security for his family.

In order to cope with this conflict and confusion, men become methodical, almost mechanical, at the time of their grief. They may often appear calm and withdrawn, shouldering their burden quietly, "like a man." They subdue emotions, trying to provide balance and comfort to those around, keeping hopes and reality in check, while crying inwardly.

There is an isolating loneliness that surround the grieving. They yearn for contact—yet withdraw from it, as if protecting themselves from a potential hurt. The prospect of getting close holds the threat of separation that becomes magnified into some awesomely scary monster.

When an older child dies, the father is left with the memories of times and events shared. But additional days and years remain void of memories. As long as a father lives, his child of 30, 40, or 50 years continues to be his child. In the event of an older child's death, the father is expected to assume tasks that he may feel ill-equipped to handle, such as providing support and guidance to grandchildren, in-law involvement, maintenance of two homes and families. His mourning is not made easier by additional burdens. However, he is usually overlooked when consolation is doled out.

It is a cruel paradox that just at this particularly painful time when they need each other most, a father often experiences isolation and estrangement from his wife.

Although both parents have endured the same loss, they don't necessarily grieve in the same way or at the same rate. Often, a man returns to the public eye; his silence regarding his mourning is misconstrued as indifference or lack of feelings.

Because of the see-saw effect of grieving, the partnership is in a constant state of confusion. When one partner is up, the other is down. This may lead to feelings of misunderstanding and lack of caring. There may be self-blame and each parent may think the other is blaming him or her. Regardless of how unrealistic and untrue this may be, the need to clarify and discuss this is clear. If left to fester, this becomes an additionally painful and isolating feeling.

The father usually feels the need to move on and not to discuss the dead child for fear of making "things" worse for his mate. His mate often experiences this as uncaring and distancing. This lack of togetherness only serves to exacerbate the already excruciating situation.

Each partner may remind the other of the missing child they once had. Sexual contact frequently diminishes. The fear of another child dying can create an anxiety which may contribute to this problem.

In our society men have been conditioned not to express emotions. In a grieving situation, this can be extremely detrimental to the ventilation of feelings; a necessary step in the progress to healing and resolution.

We reward a man who acts out his grieving in far less healthy ways—drinking, competing, working, and avoiding—by simultaneously critising him for not being expressive, compassionate, talkative, and understanding.

This process begins in early childhood when as a boy he stumbles, falls, and scrapes his knee. He comes running to his protector and all too often is ordered to stop crying like a girl.

He quickly learns to put the "cap" on and not be a "sissy" or "cry baby."

From the early age of 1 or 2 years a male child is treated as though his pain doesn't hurt. This struggle continues in the school yard, where tears from a punch, a kick, or rejection on the athletic field are met with ridicule and embarrassment. As life evolves for the male species, competitive and aggressive nature is encouraged and accepted but sensitive behavior is suspect. When pain encompasses a man's heart he remembers the discounting and condemning messages that say "cap those feelings" or risk labeling. Men, therefore, frequently have to deny their pain—demonstrating the well-learned appropriate behavior for the occasion. Society can be a demanding dictator of acceptable behavioral norms according to gender. Males are trained to be good sports when they lose; to "handle it" like a man; "to grin and bear it"; and to think logically, but not to feel emotionally.

This societal conditioning is reinforced consistently through the media, the school systems, and the family dynamics. The shell containing a man is made of granite, until a severe tragedy forces him to crack the walls himself—a task of awesome magnitude.

Is it any wonder, then, that a male who has lost a brother or sister, a child, or mate, mother, or father, finds himself stuck in his cocoon of loneliness, pain, and sadness?

Psychotherapy can be a vital part of the grieving and healing process. The therapist provides a place for the father to unleash his feelings of pain and disbelief, to share his dreams that will not come true, to open his questioning. Active listening and gentle probing are crucial to recovery, providing a safe place for the client to unburden himself of his rage and anger. Permission to "let go" is important. Often men respond successfully to saying good-bye to their child in the security of a nonjudgmental therapist. It is important in the therapeutic setting to listen to what the person is not saying. Frequently fathers feel guilty and disguise their belief that they could or should have done something more. Active listening can uncover this well-kept secret and thereby provide relief.

With the passage of time, the father's grief will eventually lessen. However, we as psychotherapists must recognize that the grieving process continues throughout a lifetime. It is one of the factors that mold and shape people into the individuals they become.

In response to the question, "How long did it take you to get over the death?" one father told me, "If you mean how long did it take me to resume a normal life, a year or two. But if you mean how long did it take to stop wishing it didn't happen, to not think about my baby, to not miss him, then I'll never be over it."

The stories go on. The issue is to recognize that a man's grieving and mourning is to be expected, encouraged, and listened to. Angry tears are essential. Ventilation is a necessary part of healing.

As professionals who are working with men who are grieving, we are presented with a challenge. We must assume responsibility for our own feelings, and offer comfort and understanding by helping the bereaved person live through the stages of grieving: denial, disbelief, anger, bargaining, depression, acceptance, and reconstruction of life without that precious child.

Vietnam Grief: Psychotherapeutic and Psychohistorical Implications

Edward Tick

ABSTRACT. A consideration of grief and grieving from the perspectives of the Vietnam War veterans, noncombatant servicemen, and a war resister. Specific therapeutic suggestions are made to ward off psychic numbness, depression, inner emptiness, and despair. Beyond an exploration of Vietnam era wounds, the author extends his conclusions to include psychohistoric factors affecting the United States people.

APPROACHING VIETNAM GRIEF

Vietnam grief is the deep inner anguish, the heaviness upon the spirit, of men and women who inevitably and unwittingly participated in an extreme, atrocious, and inescapable historical situation. In therapeutic situations with Vietnam-era clients, whether they are combat veterans, noncombatant servicemen and women, draft resisters, conscientious objectors, or others whose lives were in some significant way bound up with the Vietnam War, such prolonged and intensive grief, such heaviness of spirit, is likely to be upon them that they are not able to experience more nourishing and present-day feelings.

The word grief derives from the Latin *gravis,* meaning heavy, and originally meant heaviness of spirit. It now carries connotations of affliction, loss, sorrow. In understanding and treating grief, we must seek to know what burden it is that is heavy upon a person's spirit, that weighs a person down so much that he or she is in keen suffering or in distress. Prolonged or denied grief, grief that is neither experienced nor shared, that is especially intensive, or that is unmitigated by contrasting images of joy, nurturance, or relief, can all cause psychic suffering and wounding beyond ordinary mourning. Any or all of these forms may be present when considering Vietnam grief.

Combat veterans and other Vietnam-era clients needing to do grief work are likely to be in a condition of what Robert Jay Lifton (1970,

---

Edward Tick, Ph.D., practices psychotherapy at Chatham Psychotherapy Center. He is also a poet and is serving as president of the Hudson Valley Writers Guild. His mailing address is 714 Myrtle Ave., Albany, NY 12208.

101

1973) calls psychic numbness. Psychic numbness occurs when one is "intellectually aware of death and suffering but emotionally desensitized to them." Its purpose "is the warding off of anxiety about death and of guilt toward the dead and dying" (1970, pp. 222-3) and is likely to "merge into longer term feelings of depression and despair" (1970, p. 127). Further, such clients are likely to feel frozen not only in affect but in developmental progress, unable to mature beyond the point at which their numbing set in. This state of both affective and developmental arrest is the condition in which therapists are likely to first encounter Vietnam-era clients in whom, among other issues, the grieving process appears incomplete, distorted, chronic, or frozen.

Two major perspectives on grief in contemporary psychological literature are important to keep in mind as we consider Vietnam grief. The first is the work of Elisabeth Kübler-Ross (1969, 1978). She has demonstrated the importance of grieving as a natural and necessary psychological process with several component stages and emotions. She demonstrates that dying individuals and their families must pass through the entire grieving process in order for their heaviness to be lifted and for both the dying and those surviving them to accept their losses with equanimity. "Those who have not been able to externalize their fears and frustrations, their guilts, and their unfinished business, remain stuck in them," Kübler-Ross (1978) writes. To avoid being stuck, it is necessary for clients "to scream and rage, if necessary, to question God, to share their pain and agony" (pp 14-15).

It is not only in the confrontation of one's own death or the death of a loved one that grieving is necessary. A more controversial perspective on the necessity to grieve has been presented in the recent work of Alice Miller (1981, 1983). She holds that psychotherapy clients need not only gain insight into their conditions and not only reexperience long-buried emotions relating to their original families' insensitive or abusive treatment of them. Further, Miller insists, in order to free the self from being stuck in early emotional patterns and to prevent the repetition of such patterns throughout adult life, therapy clients must grieve. They must grieve their past traumatic treatment as well as the ideal nurturing that will never be. "The aim of analysis . . . is . . . to enable him [the client] to confront his own fate and his mourning over it" (1981, p. 102). Such grieving is necessary in order to release the self from long-contained heaviness of spirit. "Mourning is . . . an expression of pain that things happened as they did and that there is no way to change the past . . . . Sorrow reactivates numbed feelings" (1983, p. 251). Only then can the self become free of the numbness that has created the long-term condition of depression and despair and thus open to receive the love and nurturance available in present life, including from the therapist. Miller suggests that such confrontation and expression is the only way to escape a repetition compulsion—whether in the life of an individual or of a nation.

These ideas related to grief and grieving are profoundly applicable to clients suffering Vietnam-related disorders. All too often, our political leaders encourage us to "put Vietnam behind us" without examining it, certainly without feeling it. Atrocity and loss stories, when taken at face value, can leave an overwhelmingly dark impression of the human race or of the American society that perpetrated them. One does want to turn away, saying, "If this is what we are and what we do, I do not want to see."

To help heal Vietnam grief, it is the therapist's duty not to turn away. Rather, by facing squarely the terrible and ultimate losses, by bringing to the surface the overwhelmingly painful feelings against which psychic numbness is the defense, by allowing the self to grieve, and by providing the grieving self with a supportive environment in which to grieve, some lives mutilated by the Vietnam War might be freed of their burdens and enabled to flourish.

In what follows, we will examine stories of passage through the Vietnam years selected because of their grief components. We will look beneath the numbness and alienation of representative combat veterans, noncombatant servicemen, and a war resister in order to gain a sense of the place Vietnam grief has in contributing to their depression, inner emptiness, and despair. These latter conditions characterize so many of the walking wounded of the Vietnam era. In addition, we will examine not only their wounds but also what they indicate psychohistorically regarding the wounds of our nation.

Can we touch the grief of the wounded? Can they be allowed, or allow themselves, to grieve, and so melt their frozen hearts and come alive once more?

WARRIORS' GRIEF

Certain experiences can be so extremely beyond the normal range of anything we in daily life ever experience that it is impossible for people who have been through them to return to that daily life, to feel normal again. These experiences create in the survivor "the sense of having been compelled to take on this special category of existence, by which they felt permanently bound . . . [T]he experience, with all its consequences, is so profound that it can virtually become the person." To this kind of encounter, "there is, psychologically speaking, no end point, no resolution" (Lifton, 1970, pp. 143, 144, 151).

A few weeks after beginning therapy, Ben spoke about the Christmas season surrounding us. He saw the gaily decorated shopping malls, visited the department stores and watched kids sit on Santa's lap. He drove beneath the tinsel stars and bells hanging from lampposts. He had the sense of being removed, in a strange world that had and could have nothing to do with him. He retreated to his apartment to sit in darkness and silence by himself, waiting for the season to pass.

All the signs of mourning—weeping, wailing, beseeching, moaning, "the seemingly unquenchable and almost totally unsettling yearning for the return to life" (Shneidman, 1980, p. 182)—were absent. I knew the severe damage certain Vietnam veterans had incurred. Ben's state of shock, numbness, absence of affect, and self-conscious withdrawal from life were my clues that he was one of its severe victims. Early in therapy I thought that if he would only grieve—cry, wail, moan, rage, beg—there would be some hope. If we could open the pain so that his inner life, frozen like an arctic waste, could move again, then he might become human once more. But the more we talked, the more impossible that seemed, for every story he told me pointed progressively to situations of deeper grief, deeper anguish, than he could bear feeling.

First Ben told me of how he was one of ten survivors of a batttalion ambushed on a supposedly secure mountainside. While he and nine companions were holding up in a cave, he had heard the screams of dying GIs in the jungle outside; GIs were often tortured in order to bait others for the kill. Ben was reduced to helplessness in which he could only defend himself, wait, and listen to the screams. It took a week for evacuation helicopters to fly in. He and the nine sprinted for the chopper. Only he and two others made it.

"What did you see?" "How did you feel?" "Did you know any guys outside the cave?" " What did you say to each other in the cave?" "Can you remember their names now?" "What would you say to them if they were with us here, in the office?" For Ben, intellectual exercises all. He could answer me with words, but his memory resisted and, in his case, words were heartless, unattached to the visible world.

We proceeded slowly, one step at a time—a luxury he could not have had in Vietnam. But throughout our work together, he proceeded as if he might lose me at any moment, as he had his Vietnam comrades. Though he did not show any emotion, I had the sense that he feared losing me and that he introduced his stories only at a pace he believed I could bear—an unconscious protection against further loss.

Ben's narrative of jungle combat was vague. His stories seemed to run together like detached scenes from a plotless movie. Each stood out in stark relief, independent of others, brutal in impact but possessing no continuity. It was as if his sense of his own individual life as a continuous journey had been blown apart. What was left were unforgettable fragments. As Lifton (1973) summarizes, "prior images of continuity are shattered in these men" (p. 20). In Miller's terms, such fragmentation accompanies a loss of self.

Approaching a "secure" village, Ben stepped through the treeline. Suddenly sniper fire burst from the window of the nearest hut. He and his squad hit the ground, firing blasts from their M-16s, making the hut's walls "look like swiss cheese." Then they charged. Ben reached the window, threw his gun muzzle over the ledge, and looked in. In the middle of the floor was a trapdoor and in the corner not a sniper but a bleeding child. Ben ran into the hut and applied mouth-to-mouth resuscitation. The child died under him.

Ben was in a jungle camp around which patrols had secured a perimeter. His lieutenant went for a short walk, only a few hundred yards away. This lieutenant was unlike other West Pointers, without old-style glory on his mind. He just wanted himself and his men to survive. Consequently, he was loved in return by his men. When he did not return from his walk, Ben led a scouting party. In the jungle just out of sight of the camp, they found their lieutenant—naked, hanging by his outstretched arms between two trees. His severed head lay on the ground between his legs.

"That did something to us," was all Ben could say about it. No feelings, thoughts, or discussion. It just "did something." He and his squad went marauding, returning to their camp only when each of them was wearing a necklace of ears.

"How did you get the ears?" "From whom?" "How did you feel taking an ear?" "How do you feel now?" "What was it like to wear a necklace of ears?" "Can you see yourself in your mind's eye wearing that necklace? What do you look like?" "How do you feel now about what you did then?" "What would your lieutenant say?" "What do you want to say to him?"

Ben expressed no anger, guilt, sorrow—no grief.

His patrol was ambushed. Rapid fire from all sides, from the trees above. They hit the ground but the bullets were coming from everywhere. He needed cover. The man in front of him was bleeding. He crawled to the man's crumpled body, hid behind it. He heard the bullets thwacking into his friend's torso. "When I took cover, I didn't know if the man was alive or dead."

"If he were sitting here with us, what would you say?"

Expressionless, deadpan, automatic, "Thanks."

Because of experiences like these, Ben was wild, enraged, wanting to kill every Vietnamese who crossed his path. He was brought before a military psychiatric board and told that he had been in the jungle too long. His mind was no longer Western. He had begun to think, feel, act like an Oriental. He was reassigned to a company in the far north, near and in the Demilitarized Zone. No one from that unit had ever returned to the States.

"How did you feel about that? How do you live with it today? Your commanders were supposed to help you, to protect you, but instead you were sent out to be killed."

He shrugged his shoulders. "I don't know," was all he could say.

Ben is not supposed to be alive, not supposed to carry these stories. They were supposed to be blown up or buried back there, where their images could not infiltrate the rest of us in our shopping malls and offices.

But he did return. Off base, in a bar in Texas, someone picked a fight. He does not remember how or why it happened, but he killed the man. He spent a year in the stockade for manslaughter.

"How did you feel?" "What can you remember about the man?" "Did you know you were back in the States?" "How do you live with it now?"

"I don't go to bars."

Ben never once moaned, groaned, yelled, or cried in our three years of work together. At times, my own tears trickled. I left them in my eyes, on my cheeks, hoping my human reaction could be an appropriate model for grieving. In these sessions, I knew firsthand the accuracy of Lifton's observation that psychic numbing is a defense against overwhelming feelings of grief and despair. I understood why Ben could not allow himself to feel, why he was grateful that the V.A. hospital provided him with 24 pills a day. "I have a rage inside me. If I ever let that rage out, I couldn't control myself. I might kill anybody near me. And I don't want to hurt anybody ever again."

I believed him. And I believed that there was more than rage in his frozen heart. I could hear it in the way he talked about his memories. In Vietnam, he thought the necklace of ears was justified, even funny. But here and now, he was ashamed and guilty, and so living on the edge of the possibility of grieving. He had not told anyone else that story; it had been hard to tell me. He wondered if I could possibly, nonjudgmentally understand.

The dead child in the hut came up over and over again. After his act of slaughter—the spraying of the hut with M-16 rounds—Ben's first imulse had been to save the child. He often could not sleep for wondering if it had been his rounds that killed the child. He hated the Viet Cong for so using children. He also hated America for putting him in a situation where he was forced to so use children. He seemed to grieve that child but could never release the grief through tears or rage. Rather, he was permanently symbolically bound up with the slaughtered child as his indelible mark of Cain, as, perhaps, the child in himself who lost his innocence in a most devastating way, the child he could not save and whose memory he could not expunge through grieving.

He also remembered his dead lieutenant fondly. He had wanted that man to make it. What had hapened to him was profane. "It made us crazy," he said on numerous occasions. I thought of Shakespeare's King Lear, who said, "This grief hath craz'd my wits."

These clues to his feelings pockmarked our work together. I always felt, if I could just stay with him long enough, touch him deeply enough, one day he might burst into a rage or a flood of tears, mourning his lieutenant and the child and the friends he left behind. One day he would finally grieve. These thoughts were the inner dialogue of my own grief at not bridging the gap between myself and this peer.

Ben decided not to grieve. He was grateful, for therapy enabled him to begin socializing again and to date for the first time in years. He did feel a bit more a part of the human race. But he asked me not to push therapy to the point that threatened his numbness, that would wean him from his pills and enable him to feel. He had, somewhere deep within, decided that he could never again be a fully functioning member of the human race. Used up by age 22, he said, "the government pays me $18,000 a year tax free to stay this way." Perhaps his deepest unspoken grief was for his own wasted life, symbolized by the child and the lieutenant, but never released, never redeemed.

Not all combat veterans are as permanently traumatized. John came to therapy for alcoholism and marital problems. He, too, had an inner rage which he anesthetized with alcohol instead of with pills. But he let me get closer, reporting his Vietnam experiences with a hunger for someone to listen, usually drinking less as he confessed more, occasionally drinking more as his feelings got too close. We had a breakthrough when, during a flashback, he relived the death of his best friend. After 3 years together, they were on traffic control in a secure zone. John ducked into the bunker for two cups of coffee. He and Clyde drank together, exchanging small talk. Clyde handed John his empty cup and John turned to carry them back to the bunker. Just then a shot rang out. John, mere yards away, spun to see Clyde's head smashed open by the sniper's bullet.

Then, he did not cry. He hit the dirt, returned fire, tried to nurse his friend. But now, after 20 years (he had been among the first troops in Vietnam), he screamed through tears, "Ten seconds earlier and it would have been me! I didn't want him to die! It should have been me!" Finally, after 20 years of containing his grief, John reexperienced banished feelings of anger and sorrow in the present. This enabled him to mourn his lost best friend. As of this writing, John has not had a drink in 2 years.

There are one and a half million other men like Ben and John, half of whom suffer post-traumatic stress disorder.

SERVICEMEN'S GRIEF

Rod arrived for his first therapy session on a huge Harley Davidson motorcycle. He strutted into the office wearing a black helmet, black t-shirt with a skull and crossbones, black leather wristbands studded with metal spikes, black boots, and sunglasses that reflected my image back to me. Here was a walking death.

Rod "lived life in the fast lane." He frequented dangerous bars, purposely picking fights to "get the meanness out," rode with other bikers "looking for trouble." He abused drugs and alcohol, did not care if his career went anywhere, could not maintain relationships with women and, basically, treated the world with contempt. Contempt, explains Miller (1980), "is the best defense against a breakthrough of one's own feelings of helplessness: it is an expression of this split-off weakness" (p. 67).

Why did Rod want therapy? "I've got the shakes. The Doc said I'd better see you. And I have nightmares. They don't let me sleep."

Rod's shakes were anxiety attacks, coming on him unexpectedly and, as far as he could tell, untriggered by present circumstances. His nightmares were of something he called "The Beast"—a giant black thing, sometimes a horseman, sometimes a grotesque creature, sometimes a figure like Scrooge's Ghost of Christmas Future. He had escaped it for too long, but soon it would get him. Almost every night, he awoke drenched in sweat, once more having just barely evaded the beast's death grip extending toward his throat, eyes, heart.

Rod had been brought up in a nearby city, on its "mean streets." He learned to survive by fist-fighting, fast running, manipulating. His early life taught him one basic lesson: Be tough; don't feel; survive by your own moxie and wits.

During Vietnam, Rod was in the army. Contemptuous of authority, he played his cards so that he landed stateside service and a desk job. But he could not play them perfectly. Rod's job, on a New Jersey base, became routing the orders of men who had to leave for Vietnam and routing those who returned by way of his base.

"I'd get to know guys in the barracks. We'd drink together, laugh together. Then, a day or a week later, I'd march over to them and hand them their orders. You dudes are going to Nam. You others are going to Hawaii. Every time, I stayed behind." Believing he was escaping dangerous service, Rod thought the joke was on everyone else.

His duty began to be unbearable as he received some of the men shipped back. Walking through the base hospital, he viewed men without legs, arms, or eyes; men whose faces were bandaged and who had to talk through an airhole; men connected to complicated machines to keep them alive. He recognized some as men whose orders he had delivered months earlier. But the worst of it was, "I knew, every time I walked that corridor, that I might look down and see one of my buddies from home. I developed this fear of looking, knowing one day it was going to be someone I knew."

Here Rod experienced anticipatory grief, knowing he could not forever escape being touched by the war. He was also developing a guilt that would not let him rest in his self-protective contempt. He could not become completely numb, could not destroy all feelings for the war's victims and the mangled victim in himself. He began abusing drugs to resist those feelings.

"Contempt as a rule will cease with the beginning of mourning for the irreversible that cannot be changed" (Miller, 1981, p. 104). Slowly, Rod stripped his armor. The glasses and helmet came off. The mototcycle was replaced by a car. Feelings he had used LSD in the army to avoid began to surface. First was rage. It was easy to sublimate all his feelings into a blind rage; he had learned to do that well as a child. But he realized his rage was powerless against the beast. Rage gave way to fear that the beast would get him, that there was a bed and machines meant for him. His unshielded eyes grew wider, as if they would burst from his head. He began to remember the faces of the men he had seen.

He was flooded with guilt. "It could have been me. How could I escape that way? Why did I have the smarts and not them? What right did I have to stay home and land a cushy job? I hated America for that war, those guys for being stupid enough to get clobbered, myself for avoiding the whole damn thing."

Finally, his guilt gave way. There was strain in his face. He asked me, during one session, "Please, please, be the beast." He had to confront the monster before it consumed him.

I sat across from him, searching my own heart. He begged, "What do you want from me? Why are you after me?" I was coming for him. He couldn't escape me any longer. As he opened to dialogue with the beast, I became quieter, sadder. He expressed willingness to accept the beast. The beast expressed its need of him. He agreed that he owed the beast something. The beast said it wanted to collect on the overdue debt. Finally, gripping his chair, clenching his teeth, he asked, "Who are you? What is your name?" The beast replied, "I am your heart." His face broke and tears flooded his eyes. "What do you want from me?" he asked. The beast answered "A home."

Beneath Rod's rage was fear. Beneath his fear was guilt. But beneath his guilt, at the base of it all, was grief—grief for the child who had not been loved, for the country he had only wanted to fool, for all the men he helped ship to Vietnam and for the mangled men who returned; and deep grief for himself who thought he could avoid being part of a war he did not like and who, after all, became an unwitting participant in that war. Rod's armor was shed. The beast could come home. A face that was twisted in contained pain finally eased through tears.

Rod is only one of 6.5 million men who were stationed in the service in places other than Vietnam. An additional one million were stationed in Vietnam but were not in combat. These men carry another kind of burden. To be part of a war machine but not a warrior is a strange and ambiguous position. Don was stationed on a safe air base south of Saigon. During his 6 months in that country, his base was shelled only once, one man wounded. But Don returned from Vietnam to become a hermit for the next 14 years, feeling somehow separate from the human race, unworthy, unapproachable and unlovable. Because of his participation, he carries a burden of grief he cannot seem to release. In a poem he recently composed for Christmas, he wrote,

> We sent me to that war in Vietnam.
> I've seen some suffering I find
> hard to bear myself
> and hard to bear to you.
>
> I'll try not to cry
> these words when I speak
> I came back from that place
> and said I'd rather die
> than again cooperate in calculated killing.

The grief Don carries is that he was, albeit unwittingly, part of a war machine that tried to kill as many Vietnamese as efficiently as possible. Don was merely a cog in that huge machine. But he lives as if in a permanent state of grief for that small part he played.

A RESISTER'S GRIEF

This is a report on a therapy in progress. Because of the unique example of a war resister showing symptoms of post-traumatic stress and stepping forward to request treatment as one of the Vietnam War's victims, it is critical to allow this man to speak of his suffering and grief. This is especially so because it is not fashionable for us to admit that other American youth besides the combat veteran were mortally wounded by the war era. But the full extent of the damage to all factions of the generation has yet to be acknowledged.

During his years at a rural high school, while his friends made speeches condoning US actions in Southeast Asia, Sam made unpopular speeches against the war. After high school, instead of going to college, Sam dedicated himself to working on behalf of the anti-war movement.

Though Gandhi and Martin Luther King, Jr. were his role models, Sam believed that he did not have sufficient religious background to obtain a conscientious-objector status. When his draft notice came, he decided to resist induction.

Found guilty of draft evasion, Sam was sentenced to 4 years in federal prison. He then made a key decision that proved to be critical in its impact. Wanting to follow in the footsteps of Gandhi and King, holding that active nonviolence might be the only hope for our troubled world, Sam believed he should go to prison willingly. He also admitted to himself that he could not withstand 4 years in prison. Instead, he went underground.

He made his way to Canada, where he adopted an assumed identity. While there, he lived in the constant fear that at any moment an agent would kick down his door and drag him back to prison. He believes he developed a conditioned paranoia that has never left him. After 6 years, he decided to return under Ford's clemency program.

Since returning, Sam has worked with psychiatric patients, but maintains no friendships outside work. His marriage is troubled and he lives in almost complete isolation from others, "the only way I feel complete." Most of the time, Sam exhibits the same psychic numbness that characterizes so many veterans. He believes that he has feelings buried deeply inside him, but that he cannot possibly allow these feelings to surface. He would find the grief over his own fate and the fate of the world too much to bear. Instead of experiencing strong feelings, Sam exhibits a constant state of quiet, withdrawn, subdued mourning.

> I do mourn what has happened to me personally. I've lost the chance to be intimate, to be united with anyone else, un-alone and therefore spiritually at rest in a cold universe. For me, one of the primary truths that emerged from the Vietnam era is that words cannot facilitate intimacy. . . . Only shared experience can do that. And my experience during Vietnam was so strange and out of the ordinary, that . . . for all practical purposes, no one else did go through it.
>
> The principal experience of my youth and young manhood was the fugitive's experience. I was also an exile, in flight from justice. Not that unusual so far. . . . The thing about me is: In hiding and running all those years, I believe that I became a failure as a moral and ethical man. . . . When I returned to the States . . . , one of the Vietnam veterans who met me said, "You look like you just came out of the bush." He sensed that something wasn't right with me. But he quickly brushed that intuition away by adding, "What could be the matter? *You* did what you thought was *right*." But I didn't. . . . Veterans, lovers, therapists heard what I had to say. And none of them could understand. . . . That's how it is with me. I have not been understood on the most crucial period of my life. I do not try to be understood when it comes to lesser events. . . .
>
> I am alone. Intimacy is not possible. That is why I grieve.

Sam expresses a loss of self because of the loss of the possibility of mutuality. He believes that in failing to go to prison, he became "a failure as a moral and ethical man," and grieves his lost integrity. This prevents him from advancing into mature adulthood. "My best friend [a combat veteran] and I are both stuck at age 19. I don't know any way to grow past it. I have only an ounce of hope that we can ever mature."

Sam fears his integral self is already dead. He is grieving that part of his ideal self that was never given the chance to live—either by his withdrawn, nonaffirming parents; his society that demanded either the unethical or imprisonment; or by his own self prematurely and in isolation striving to emulate King and Gandhi.

Sam affirms that he is "a modern man," in existential anguish over the isolation and absurdity of human life in a cold universe. As World War II did for the French existentialists, Vietnam for Sam portrayed our civilization's ultimate amorality and folly. Because of this, Sam seems afflicted with a heaviness of spirit that is beyond his years and beyond his individual experiences. It is as if he were mourning the exiled child never recognized by his parents, the generational fragment of truly moral youth never recognized by the Kennedy-Johnson-Nixon governments at war, and the fugitive post-modern individual alone in an increasingly violent and repressive world. In each, the pattern is the same. Because of each, Sam is grieving.

Yet there is a stuck component to his grief. He does not cry or rage, but rather succumbs. In this sense, he is not passing through Kübler-Ross' stages, but resisting active mourning. In Miller's (1981) words,

> avoiding this mourning means that one remains at bottom the one who is despised. For I have to despise everything in myself that is not wonderful, good and clever. Thus I perpetuate intrapsychically the loneliness of childhood: I despise weakness, impotence, uncertainty—in short, the child in myself and in others. (p. 103)

Sam felt despised not only as a child, but as a war resister—an American youth who tried to be good, wonderful beyond his years and abilities, and was condemned for even that.

To date, Sam is progressing in therapy to the point where he is, for the first time, beginning to allow mutuality to exist. Unable to build bridges himself, he is cooperating with the building of a "tenuous" bridge between himself and his therapist. As that primal bridge is constructed, he slowly, tentatively, is beginning to construct bridges outside the therapy relationship—significantly, to combat veterans. After 6 years in exile and many more in withdrawn isolation, Sam's self is beginning to return home.

PSYCHOHISTORICAL IMPLICATIONS

I am a member of the Vietnam generation. I escaped service, as did so many of my middle-class peers, through college deferments and then the lottery system. During the war years, I watched the approaching end of college with dread, protesting the war with anger and innocence, feared the future and struggled to make a decision that gave me some control over it. Fear, doubt, and uncertainty about my coming of age lingered for many years, and though history made it possible for me to escape personal anguish, I have never felt that I escaped clean.

Elsewhere I have documented my reactions to such a coming of age (Tick, 1985a, 1985b). Suffice it to say here that part of my way of coping with my nonparticipation and moral ambiguity is found in my chosen profession. As a professional healer, I can work with some of the wounds caused by that historical situation and my country.

Such healing is never easy. It means, I have learned, listening to many of the stories that many like Sam did their youthful and ineffectual best to prevent. It demands building bridges with men who lived through different worlds, who may, initially, hate or mistrust me. It necessitates, at times, going to war, if only in my imagination, and learning what was done to these men and to the Vietnamese. It means living with the awareness that for all my good wishes and intentions, horrors beyond speaking were committed in my country's name. Some people know it and many were crippled by it. Finally, it means that I am growing a seething, steady rage at the continued rewriting of history, the continued denial and cover-up, that can be found in recent American political policy and public and media events. These demands and necessities I am willing to accept and struggle with; they expose and express my own grief as a member of the Vietnam generation. And they affirm this critical perspective: a therapist, a wounded healer, must be willing to grieve, with all that that demands, in order to help heal an individual, a generation, a nation.

Somehow, all of America must learn to cry. The men I work with carry grievous wounds and tales. Whether as combat veterans, as servicemen, or as resisters, they have seen things, known things, that make "business as usual" impossible. They must not carry their grief alone. What our country did in Vietnam was the result not merely of individual actions, but of a collective wound that causes us to perpetrate wars such as Vietnam, to deny the true costs of such wars, to adopt a bullying and superior attitude toward people and systems different from our own. Our only chance to heal is to open the pain that is in all of us, to see what we truly do, what we, before the eyes of humanity, are responsible for.

In ancient myths, warriors did not shirk paying their debts. Rather, they mourned their victims, did obeisance before their memories, paid with head-hanging service for taking life. There are, for example, many prayers among Native Americans for the soul of a slain enemy. And, more recently, after one of the Arab-Israeli wars, Golda Meir said, "I can forgive you for killing my children. What I cannot forgive is your making a killer of me."

It is not humanly possible to kill lightly, without grief, especially when lacking a moral basis for the killing. As M. Scott Peck (1983) wrote, "If we must kill, let us honestly suffer the agony involved ourselves. Otherwise we will insulate ourselves from our own deeds, and as a whole people we will become . . . evil. For evil arises in the refusal to acknowledge our own sins" (pp. 232-3). Having killed, we are psychohistorically responsible to grieve. To refuse to grieve is to dehumanize ourselves and to become evil.

I am convinced that there is a grief beyond anything we have yet uncovered that lies, not merely at the heart of the Vietnam experience, but at the heart of the American experience. The homelessness, the restlessness, the constant imposition of our power over the lives of others, the tendency to bully, to use violence to get our ways—these strategies we see repeated again and again throughout American history. Thus, by working with the wounded of the Vietnam era, I am not only a therapist. I also become a witness to what the collective American psyche can do if it is not healed. The consequences of an unhealed superpowerful psyche acting out its pain upon the world are too terrible to contemplate. As with an individual, so with a nation—healing can only occur if we grieve.

People cannot grieve in a vacuum. In all religions and societies, mourners are supported by a grieving community. But the victims of Vietnam are left alone, unsupported by the American community at large in their grief. They are like the ancient azazel, the scapegoat, that had the sins of its community tied around its neck and was then shooed out into the desert to die. The community believed that the suffering and death of the scapegoat expiated their sins, thus alleviating their need to grieve.

We can deny, but we cannot alleviate, the need to grieve. The Vietnam War is not over. It is walking the streets of our cities, dwelling in the homes of our families, sleeping in the beds of our neighbors. Our nation cannot banish our sins with either scapegoats or the further acting out of violence. Nor can we delegate to therapists alone the responsibility to heal those whom we as a society have condemned. Not only Vietnam victims, but the entire Vietnam experience, must be accepted into the consciousness of America for what it was. As an individual, Rod accomplished this with his beast. But beyond what can happen in the therapy setting, our national responsibility must be faced in all its horror and felt until we are not ashamed of our tears. Personal and national change can only occur through experiencing grief. Like some of the wounded who finally, after 10 or 20 years, learn to cry, we should wear our tears before the world—proud that we can cry, in humility, in expiation.

REFERENCES

Kübler-Ross, E. (1969). *On death and dying.* New York: Macmillan.
Kübler-Ross, E. (1978). *To live until we say goodbye.* Englewood Cliffs, NJ: Prentice-Hall.
Lifton, R. J. (1970). *History and human survival.* New York: Random House.

Lifton, R. J. (1973). *Home from the war.* New York: Simon and Schuster.

Miller, A. (1981). *Prisoners of childhood.* New York: Basic Books.

Miller, A. (1983). *For your own good.* New York: Farrar, Straus, Giroux.

Peck, M. S. (1983). *People of the lie.* New York: Simon & Schuster.

Schneidman, E. (1980). *Voices of death.* New York: Harper & Row.

Tick, E. (1985, Jan. 13). Apocalypse Continued. *The New York Times Magazine,* p. 60.

Tick, E. (in press). Vietnam, alienation and the motivation to heal. *Voices: The art and science of psychotherapy.*

The Grieving Patient in Later Life

T. L. Brink

ABSTRACT. Reviews different forms of loss and grief in later life: widowhood, chronic physical disability, and retirement. Notes differences (e.g., severity, duration, stages) between older and younger individuals in their experiences of grief. Contends that geriatric psychopathology is largely comprised of dementia, depression, hypochondriasis, and paranoia. With the exception of dementia, these disorders are frequently secondary to grief reactions. Suggests that geriatric psychotherapy be flexible to the needs and situation of the client: the form, length, frequency, and agent must be determined by context. Offers a case study to illustrate these points.

Grief is a painful emotional state which occurs in response to a loss. Grief may occur at any point in the life cycle, but it is especially common in elders because there are so many losses in later life.

LOSS AND GRIEF IN LATER LIFE

Every phase of life involves physical, mental, interpersonal, and cultural changes that present individuals with a challenge to successful development. In later life there are three main losses, and each of these is a source of possible grieving: chronic physical disorders, widowhood, and retirement. Regardless of its origin, each loss impacts the individual on several levels: biological, psychological, and socioeconomic.

Widowhood is probably the first example of bereavement that pops into mind. It may be a problem that originates in the interpersonal dimension, but quickly becomes a psychological problem in that it strips elders of the role of spouse and also denies them stimulation (i.e., love and/or conflict). Rates of depression, hypochondriasis, paranoia, and suicide are high for the widowed (Brink, 1979). The problem also has a physical

Dr. Brink is editor of *Clinical Gerontologist: the journal of aging and mental health.* He holds faculty appointments at the College of Notre Dame (Belmont, CA), Western Graduate School of Psychology (Palo Alto, CA), and Stanford University School of Medicine, Department of Psychiatry, 1044 Sylvan, San Carlos, CA 94070.

117

dimension: Mortality rates for the widowed are much higher than those for comparable married persons.

While the death of a spouse is a major bio-psycho-social crisis for all elders, it appears to be somewhat more tragic for women. One reason for this is societal. Today's aged women grew up in a cohort in which most of them found that the role of wife and mother (rather than career builder) was their principal role. Another reason is the differential life expectancy for the sexes. The female of most species lives longer than the male. For American elders the life expectancies are 69 for men, 77 for women. Since the current elders came from a cohort where the men married younger women, it is not surprising that the average woman has over a dozen years in the role of widow. To look at it another way: two-thirds of the old men are married; only one-third of old women are married. The number of available women so greatly outnumbers the available men that few old widows can hope for remarriage, or even a steady relationship with a man.

The majority of American elders suffer from at least one *chronic physical disability,* which may range from sensory loss (poor vision or hearing), motor impairment (resulting from strokes, hip fractures, or arthritis), or systemic debilities such as heart problems or diabetes. While elders are only a ninth of the population, they constitute almost a third of the nation's health-care bill. Although these conditions have a physical origin, they quickly involve the psychological dimension as a grief reaction may emerge as body image and self-esteem deteriorate; and the social dimension as the individual is less able to initiate and respond to interpersonal contacts. The individual grieves the loss of a life-style based upon normal physical functioning.

Organic brain syndromes (i.e., dementia) are also a potential source of grief, both for patients and their families. In the early stages of mental deterioration, patients are aware that something is happening, that their minds are no longer capable of processing new information. The result is a potentially severe grief reaction superimposed on the organic mental disorder. As the disease progresses, patients usually become too confused to be aware of their condition, and the grief shifts to the family members who mourn the loss of a loved one and who must take over more and more of daily care responsibilities.

When chronic physical (or mental) disability leads to institutionalization, there are physical, mental, and social results, usually negative. The death rate of patients sent to a nursing home is high, not just because such people were sick to begin with, but also because of the bio-psycho-social stress of institutionalization and relocation. The mind becomes dulled in most nursing homes, with levels of confusion and depression increasing dramatically (Brink, 1979). Perhaps the most insidious problem with institutionalization is the disruption of established patterns of social and

familial interaction. The individual grieves the loss of the noninstitution-
alized life-style.

Retirement is a major life change, especially for men. The majority
look forward to retirement, and adjust well. However, a positive anticipation of retirement is not necessarily the best predictor of successful adjustment. The people who do the best are those who have cultivated numerous outside interests, and also those professionals who can taper off their
life's work while retaining the titles and trappings of their vocation. It is
the blue-collar worker who had little life beyond the job who adjusts most
poorly to retirement, and who is the most likely to grieve over the loss of
the vocational role.

Although retirement originates in one sphere of life, it rapidly pervades
the others. Many retirees are amazed to find how many of their social
contacts were job-related. Many homemaker spouses develop extreme
frustration having to deal with the physical presence of the new retiree in
the home 7 days a week. Some children complain of father's "meddling"
attitude since retirement.

AGE-RELATED DIFFERENCES

It is not only the nature and frequency of losses which differentiate
younger from older bereaved patients. There are also differences in the
patterns of adjustment to those losses. These differences probably hold
for all forms of grief, but they are most clear in the case of widowhood.

Severity of the bereavement reaction is reduced with advanced age
(Heyman & Gianturco, 1973; Maddison & Walker, 1967; Parkes, 1972).
At least one study found that age was the most important variable in
predicting early, successful resolution of the widow's grief (Ball, 1976).
Normal elders seem to adapt to the death of a spouse with emotional stability and few life changes (Gianturco & Busse, 1978). This may be due
to developmental factors (i.e., greater acceptance of widowhood role as
being "appropriate" for that point in the life-cycle) and cohort factors
(e.g., religiosity).

Duration of the deceased's illness is a factor in predicting the severity
and duration of the grief reaction. However, the relationship between
these variables is reversed after age 65. For younger widows (i.e., those
under age 45) the most difficult situation is when the spouse dies suddenly. For older widows, the most difficult situation is when the spouse dies a
lingering death (Vachon, 1976).

Stage models of grief have been suggested by several authors (e.g.,
Gorer, 1965; Kreis & Pattie, 1969; Spiegel, 1973; Tanner, 1976; DeVaul
& Zisook, 1976; Conroy, 1977). While these models may be useful in
working with children, adolescents, and young adults, the older the pa-

tient, the less the grief reaction fits into a prefabricated course with clearly demarcated stages. A common pattern is for there to be a gradual adjustment, with occasional lapses into a more severe grief (Parkes, 1972).

GERIATRIC PSYCHOPATHOLOGY

It is usually a grieving experience in the wake of chronic physical disability, retirement, and/or widowhood that produces most of the serious, nonorganic mental problems of later life.

Depression is similar to the blues, but is harder to shake and comes to disrupt our ability to function in daily activities. Depression is the most common mental disorder in any age group in the US today. Depression may be more widespread among elders than other aged groups (Levitt & Lubin, 1975). It is particularly widespread among the retired (Busse, 1970), those with chronic physical disability, and the recently widowed. Among patients with verifiable organic brain syndrome, between a quarter and a half have a clinically significant depressive overlay (Liston, 1977).

Diagnosis of geriatric depression is complicated by several factors. Foremost is the fact that geriatric symptomatology differs from that of younger age groups. Classic depressive symptomatology appears in three domains: affective (crying, sadness, apathy); cognitive (thoughts of hopelessness, helplessness, worthlessness, suicide, guilt); and somatic (disturbances of energy level, appetite, sleep, elimination, libido). In later life, the somatic symptoms (especially fatigue, constipation, and insomnia) lose their diagnostic specificity: nondepressed elders also have these complaints.

The therapist should not rely on what nursing-home staff say about depression in patients. Staff comprehension of, and ability to diagnose, geriatric depression varies widely, and is largely determined by training. Many late-life depressions have the classic symptoms masked by somatic disorders, physical complaints, or anger. Furthermore, depression may be acute or episodic, coming or ending abruptly; and the staff's evaluation may be based upon how the patient seemed to be doing last week.

In order to improve the diagnosis of geriatric depression, it is necessary to use assessment techniques which have been developed for, and are appropriate with, the aged. The Geriatric Depression Scale (GDS) may be the only self-rating depression test specifically devised for and standardized with elders (Brink, Yesavage, Lum, Heersema, Adey, & Rose, 1982; Yesavage, Brink, Rose, Lum, Huang, Adey, & Leirer, 1983). Unless there is severe dementia, the GDS should give an accurate picture of the level of depression (Brink, 1984).

GERIATRIC DEPRESSION SCALE

1. Are you basically satisfied with your life? N
2. Have you dropped many of your activities and interests? Y
3. Do you feel that your life is empty? Y
4. Do you often get bored? Y
5. Are you hopeful about the future? N
6. Are you bothered by thoughts that you just cannot get out of your head? Y
7. Are you in good spirits most of the time? N
8. Are you afraid that something bad is going to happen to you? Y
9. Do you feel happy most of the time? N
10. Do you often feel helpless? Y
11. Do you often get restless and fidgety? Y
12. Do you prefer to stay home at night, rather than go out and do new things? Y
13. Do you frequently worry about the future? Y
14. Do you feel that you have more problems with memory than most? Y
15. Do you think it is wonderful to be alive now? N
16. Do you often feel downhearted and blue? Y
17. Do you feel pretty worthless the way you are now? Y
18. Do you worry a lot about the past? Y
19. Do you find life very exciting? N
20. Is it hard for you to get started on new projects? Y
21. Do you feel full of energy? N
22. Do you feel that your situation is hopeless? Y
23. Do you think that most people are better off than you are? Y
24. Do you frequently get upset over little things? Y
25. Do you frequently feel like crying? Y
26. Do you have trouble concentrating? Y
27. Do you enjoy getting up in the morning? N
28. Do you prefer to avoid social gatherings? Y
29. Is it easy for you to make decisions? N
30. Is your mind as clear as it used to be? N

Administration: These items may be administered in oral or written format. If the latter is used, it is important that the answer sheet have printed YES/NO after each question, and the subject is instructed to circle the better response. If administered orally, the examiner may have to repeat the question in order to get a response that is more clearly a yes or no. The GDS loses validity as dementia increases. The GDS seems to work well with other age groups. Translations are available: Spanish, French.

Scoring: Count 1 point for each depressive answer. 0-10 = normal; 11-20 = mild depression; 21-30 = moderate or severe depression.

Over a third of all aged widows develop some depressive symptoms (Clayton, Halikas, & Maurice, 1972). "Normal" grief reactions differ from clinically significant depressions in that the latter are more likely to endorse self-deprecatory thoughts: self-blame, failure, guilt, punishment, disappointment, irritability (Gallagher, Breckenridge, Thompson, Dessonville, & Amaral, 1982). This is yet another reason why depression should be assessed by an instrument such as the GDS, which minimizes the purely somatic symptoms emphasized in the Zung and Hamilton scales.

Paranoia and hypochondriasis are delusional systems which involve false beliefs of physical illness (hypochondriasis) or the evil doings and conspiracies of others (paranoia). Both hypochondriacs and paranoids are complainers, self-excusers, and other-blamers. "It's not my fault I didn't accomplish much and I am here in this horrible housing project now." The hypochondriacs blame their mysterious physical problems for their fate; paranoids blame mysterious plots against them. Although hypochondriacs and paranoids may be encountered at any age, these disorders appear more frequently in later life, especially in patients who are demented and/or depressed. Apparently, the delusions of hypochondriasis and paranoia give patients some consolation for losses they are experiencing, and by shifting the blame to something beyond their control, paranoia and hypochondriasis serve the function of maintaining self-esteem. Also, these complaints provide some sympathy, or at least attention, from others.

You know that you are dealing with a paranoid when the accusations become incredible and obviously serve the function of explaining away the witness' own losses and shortcomings. A woman with memory loss may complain, "I can't find my cane. Somebody comes in here at night and moves it." A man who has not accepted his diminished financial status may say, "Look at this dirty old blanket on the bed. That's not my blanket. I had a good one, brand new, but someone came in here, took it, and left this old thing, but I know the difference." Usually the imaginary culprits are neighbors, the letter carrier, or nursing home staff.

Geriatric hypochondriasis should not be inferred from patient behavior alone. Many elders have so many, and such serious, physical problems that their complaints may not be delusional. A diagnosis of hypochondriasis should be made only after an extensive diagnostic workup for the reported physical symptoms or an examination of the patient's health attitudes, via a test such as the HSIG (Brink, Belanger, Bryant, Capri, Janakes, Jasculca, & Oliveira, 1978; Brink, 1984).

H.S.I.G.

Hypochondriasis Scale (Institutional Geriatric)

1. Are you satisfied with your health most of the time? N
2. Do you ever feel completely well? N
       ["Outside of this specific problem . . ." = Y]
3. Are you tired most of the time? Y
       ["I get tired a lot." = N]
4. Do you feel your best in the morning? N
       ["Always feel the same." = Y]
5. Do you frequently have strange aches and pains that you cannot
   identify? Y
       ["I know what they are." = N]
6. Is it hard for you to believe it when the doctor tells you that there is
   nothing physically wrong with you? Y
       ["He/She knows what's wrong with me" = N]

Administration: These items may be administered in oral or written format, but the former is preferred. The examiner may have to repeat a question in order to get a response that is clearly yes or no. Translations are available for Spanish and French. The HSIG seems to work well with non-institutionalized elders and also with young adults and adolescents, although no precise validity studies have been done on these other groups.

Scoring: Count one point for each hypochondriacal answer. In both the institutional and community elder populations, the modal score is 0, the median 1. This test is a measure of hypochondriacal attitudes, rather than hypochondriacal behavior. It is possible for a patient to score high (e.g., 4-6) and yet manifest no somatic complaints. Any patient who has numerous somatic complaints and scores high is probably suffering from delusional illness. Any score under 3 is definitely not hypochondriacal, and so the patient's complaints should be taken seriously.

The incidence of both paranoia and hypochondriasis is somewhat higher among the widowed than among married elders (Peretz, 1970). It is also higher among those with impaired hearing, and among the retired. One complication with the diagnosis of either of these delusional systems is the possibility that the client's complaint may have some valid basis in reality: confidence artists do conspire against the relatively helpless (e.g., recently widowed, physically disabled) and many elders do have real physical complaints. The frequency of psychosomatic disorders among the widowed is quite high (Maddison & Viola, 1968). This is yet another reason for using a test such as the HSIG, which focuses on health attitudes rather than being a mere symptom checklist.

THERAPY

There are several basic guidelines for treating bereaved elders. Perhaps the cardinal rule is *let the treatment suit the patient.* There are several key variables which may determine important aspects of treatment.

Who is the therapist of choice depends upon who it is that the client seeks out, or at least has an ease in establishing rapport with. Frequently, this will be a general-practice physician, social worker, rabbi, priest, minister, or peer rather than a psychologist or psychiatrist. Hypochondriacs are most likely to seek physicians, and are approachable only when their problem is addressed in somatic terms. Paranoids may seek police or social workers. Depressives may not actively seek out help. Whoever is first to find them and establish a trusting relationship may be the best therapist.

What type of therapy is preferable is also contextually determined. Well-educated clients, especially those with previous successful experience in therapy, may benefit from the more traditional psychodynamic or nondirective approaches. The client who is less educated, acculturated, and/or familiar with psychotherapy will do better with a more cognitive or directive approach. The more confused a client is, the more a purely behavioral approach is called for. The more structured a patient's environment is, the more likely a behavioral approach is to succeed (Hussian, 1981). The degree to which therapy should, or can, be emotionally cathartic depends upon the personality of the bereaved. Not every elder can satisfy some therapists' expectation of tears.

How the therapy takes place is also contingent upon the patient and the patient's environment. Those living alone are usually best handled in individual sessions. Those living at home with family members are prime candidates for family therapy. Those who live in semi-institutional environments have the greatest opportunity for group and milieu therapy. Those with severe communication disorders (e.g., deafness, aphasia, memory loss) may not fit into groups composed of more capable patients.

When therapy takes place (frequency) and when it is to be terminated (duration) also require a great deal of flexibility. In general, sessions should be shorter than the traditional hour and more frequent than the traditional once a week, at least during the acute stage of depression, hypochondriasis, or paranoia. One technique that may be useful with these disorders is to cut the session short when the patient returns to delusional statements (persecution in paranoia; somatic disorder in hypochondriasis; helplessless, hopelessness, guilt, and self-blame in depression). Such a behavioral technique is highly effective in getting the patient to talk about positive factors and/or real psychosocial issues (Brink, 1980).

Just *who is the client* is something that the therapist must always consider. Certainly in cases of progressive and irreversible dementia, the client becomes less and less the person with the organic brain disease, and more and more the caregivers as the grief burden is shifted. The same is the case with some intractable paranoids and hypochondriacs. The real task is to help those who have to live with the patient not to feel guilty, not to take the patient's statements personally.

A CASE STUDY

Martina A. was a 68-year-old meztizo woman, born and raised in rural Mexico. Three years ago, her husband died. Unable to maintain the tiny farm in a remote area of the state of Mexico, she moved with her oldest son to Nezahualcoyotl (a poor and crowded suburb of Mexico City) and lived with his wife and five children.

Doña Martina was unable to adjust to life in the new environment. She grieved not only the loss of her husband, but also the loss of her rural lifestyle. There simply was not enough for her to do (that she could do). She sat around and did nothing day after day. Within a few months she was severely depressed (GDS = 22) and moderately confused (only 3 right on international version of Mental Status Questionnaire, Brink, 1979).

She was seen by a general-practice physician and given a low dosage of a tricyclic antidepressant. The treatment also included six brief (10-20 minutes) therapy sessions with the physician, spread out over 2 months. During these sessions, there was some exploration of the client's feelings about her current situation, and even some reminiscence about the past. The tone of the sessions was generally directive, with the physician heavily relying upon his authority position to get Martina to reinterpret her situation and change her behavior. She left the sessions in good spirits, and seemed to eagerly anticipate them. After 4 weeks, her GDS fell to 11, and MSQ improved to 7 trials passed. These visits were terminated by mutual consent with the understanding that they could be resumed as needed by the patient.

Within a year, the family was back complaining about Doña Martina. She had gradually become more confused, insulting, angry, and paranoid. When depressed, she had been quite manageable: curling up silently in a corner. Now she accused family members and neighbors of having pilfered her jewels (which had been sold many years before) and even worthless belongings (especially those that Martina herself had misplaced in her own confusion). Although she forgot what she had just done or heard, Martina never seemed to forget the *majaderias* (swear words) she learned from her salty Mexican peasant husband.

At this time, she scored 15 the GDS (mildly depressed), but only 1 on the MSQ. Her confusion and short-term memory loss made her quite incapable of benefiting from anything that her therapist said. She proved unresponsive to the tricyclic that had worked previously. After two family therapy sessions with Martina, her son, and daughter-in-law, the physician decided to prescribe haloperidol in order to reduce Martina's level of agitation and outburst. While it was modestly successful in achieving those goals, it had no impact on her confusion or depression.

The therapist demonstrated admirable flexibility in this case. First, when it appeared that Martina could be returned to quasi-normal functioning via the alleviation of her depression, he used a combination of antidepressant medication and psychotherapy appropriate in content and format. As paranoia secondary to a progressive organic brain syndrome became the presenting problem, he altered both his prognosis and prescription to fit the new diagnosis. He shifted his emphasis from helping her return to her old self, to helping her family cope with the terminal phase of her mental death.

REFERENCES

Ball, J.F. (1976). Widows' grief: The impact of age and mode of death, *Omega, 7,* 307-333.

Brink, T.L. (1979). *Geriatric psychotherapy.* New York: Human Sciences Press.

Brink, T.L. (1980). Geriatric paranoia: A case study illustrating behavioral management. *Journal of the American Geriatrics Society, 28,* 355-359.

Brink, T.L. (1984). Limitations of the GDS. *Clinical Gerontologist 2*(3), 60-61.

Brink, T.L. (1984). Use and limitations of the HSIG. *Clinical Gerontologist, 3*(1), 68-69.

Brink, T.L., Belanger, J., Bryant, J., Capri, D., Janakes, C., Jasculca, S., & Oliveira, C. (1978). Hypochondriasis in an institutional geriatric population: Construction of a scale (HSIG). *Journal of the American Geriatrics Society 26,* 557-559.

Brink, T.L., Yesavage, J.A., Lum, O., Heersema, P., Adey, M., & Rose, T.L. (1982) Screening tests for geriatric depression. *Clinical Gerontologist, 1*(1), 37-43.

Busse, E.W. (1970) Psychoneurotic reactions and defense mechanisms. In E. Palmore (Ed.), *Normal Aging* (pp. 84-90). Durham, NC: Duke University Press.

Clayton, P.J., Halikas, J.A., & Maurice, W.L. (1972) The depression of widowhood. *British Journal of Psychiatry, 120,* 71-78.

Conroy, R.C. (1977). Widows and widowhood. *New York State Journal of Medicine, 77,* 357-360.

DeVaul, R.A., & Zisook, S. (1976). Unresolved grief. *Postgraduate Medicine, 59,* 267-271.

Gallagher, D., Breckenridge, J.N., Thompson, L.W., Dessonville, C., & Amaral, P. (1982). Similarities and differences between normal grief and depression in older adults. *Essence 5,* 127-140.

Gianturco, D.T., & Busse, E.W. (1978). Psychiatric problems encountered during a long-term study of normal aging volunteers. In A.D. Isaacs & F. Post (Eds.), *Studies in Geriatric Psychiatry* (pp. 1-17), New York: Wiley.

Gorer, G. (1965). *Death, grief, and mourning in contemporary Britain.* London: Cresset.

Heyman, D.K., & Gianturco, D.T. (1973). Long-term adaptation by the elderly to bereavement. *Journal of Gerontology, 28,* 359-362.

Hussian, R.L. (1981). *Geriatric psychology.* New York: Van Nostrand Reinhold.

Kreis, B., & Pattie, A. (1969). *Up from grief: Patterns of recovery.* New York: Seabury.

Levitt, E.E., & Lubin, B. (1975). *Depression.* New York: Springer.

Liston, E.H. (1977). Occult presenile dementia. *Journal of Nervous and Mental Disease. 164,* 263-267.

Maddison, D., & Viola, A. (1968). The health of widows the year following bereavement. *Journal of Psychosomatic Research, 12,* 297-306.

Maddison, D., & Walker, W. (1967). Factors affecting the outcome of conjugal bereavement. *British Journal of Psychiatry, 113,* 1057-1067.

Parkes, C.M. (1972). *Bereavement: Studies of adult grief.* New York: International Universities Press.

Peretz, D. (1970). Reactions to loss. In B. Schoenberg, A.C. Carr, D. Peretz & A.H. Kutscher (Eds.), *Loss and Grief: psychological management in medical practice.* New York: Columbia University Press.

Spiegel, Y. (1973). *The grief process.* Nashville: Abingdon.

Tanner, I.J. (1976). *The gift of grief.* New York: Hawthorne.

Vachon, M.L.S. (1976). Grief and bereavement following the death of a spouse. *Canadian Psychiatric Association Journal, 21,* 35-44.

Yesavage, J.A., Brink, T.L., Rose, T.L., Lum, O., Huang, V., Adey, M., & Leirer, V.O. (1983). Development and validation of a geriatric depression screening scale: A preliminary report. *Journal of Psychiatric Research, 17,* 37-49.

Living Your Dying

Stanley Keleman

ABSTRACT. In dealing with three major realms and sequence to life and death, this article examines the dying process. It suggests a supportive approach for the shedding of images of who a person "should be." The article assumes that experience itself is the ultimate teacher in these matters.

Existence is orderly and ongoing, a chain of living events connected in a way that results in a continuum and structuring of experience. We are part and parcel of that ordering process. Our experience of organizing and forming our body, starting embryologically and then emotionally and socially, is part of this. The business of somatizing is the organized crystalizing of experience into behavioral forms, to endure long enough to be our history, in the shapes which symbolize and express meaning. Embodiment, then, is the concretization of an ongoing experience, an encapsulation of the stream of existence. Without being embodied there is no perception of existence, since we would not have any experience without having a body.

Life is a process of organizing and disorganizing a sequence of events, and our embodiment partakes in that sequentialness. That is, we start as small organized structures and we form ourselves into big complex organisms, and we maintain that bigness for a while and then we internally disorganize and shrink. And that principle of the process of existence extends throughout all time and has a future as well as an ancient past. That is, the process of life, whatever its origin, has a history, a very vital present, and an all-pervasive orientation toward a future. Nature organizes and disorganizes: This process is a journey collectively, and individually— it is at the heart of the experience of human community.

If we think about life and death as an orderly process, we can see that this orderly process gives rise to meaning. There are, in the ordering of existence, the genetic programs or the imprinted experiences that sustain existence and help what has organized to also destructure itself. We begin to understand that our own life goes through a series of very vital events

Stanley Keleman has been practicing and developing somatic psychology for over 30 years. He is the author of several books, the most recent being *Emotional Anatomy* (Center Press). He maintains a private and group practice and is director of the Center for Energetic Studies in Berkeley, 2045 Francisco Street, Berkeley, CA 94709.

that lays the groundwork for the next stage of existence, be it from child to adolescent, from adult to old age, organizing the elements of experience from one form of consciousness and behavioral configurations to the next one. We begin to recognize that there is a very clear blueprint handed down to us in our genetic structure, in our psyche, and in our social and mythic traditions; that there is this universal process of organizing and disorganizing human forms.

I see three major realms and three major sequences to this process. The three realms of our experience are a prepersonal, genetic and instinctive; a post-personal, societal; and a personal, individual organization of existence. Each and every one of us has an ancient sea of molecular activity that goes back to the dawn of existence. This realm, where the universal archetypes give the basic patents of form, we can call nature. That environment, which every one of us partakes and generates as part of the nature of our existence—that great unconscious sea that animates life—in that ocean one could say that death is unknown and all there is is a perpetual sea of replication. On the next level are the social roles that primitive or advanced societies demand of us in the carrying out of our roles as parents or workers or warriors, that is, the on-goingness of organized, communal, societal life. That level of order also has a tremendous history and a tradition; that is, almost all existence forms relationships with that which is around it and that which resembles itself. So there is societal perpetuation and the society is a vital organism. And then there is that in-between world of our personal existence—the differentiated shapes we recognize as our identity—our personalized individuated identity, partitioned from the roles we play in the prepersonal or societal oceans.

Each of these realms has its own life form. When a youngster exits from the great ocean in its mother's belly, into societal existence, in those first moments in which it enters this existence you see almost a pure, prepersonal organization of life, living almost reflexively, but completely without the seed of its own individuality. As it gasps for its first breath, bringing it into the air-breathing society, it is surrounded by the participants of our society and given the support that permits it to grow, to mature toward adulthood, as well as the initiation into the gendered roles. Years later you see the unique combination of what society has formed and how the person's individuality has tried to find an expression of its uniqueness inside that society. You see the twists and the bends and the lines and the wrinkles from the use of oneself that give the mark of the individual.

These three realms play an important part in the organizing of the de-structuring, in the dying process, because two of these roles come to an end. It's in two of these roles that existence is threatened, and one that we may or may not know about, the prepersonal realm, which is in no way threatened. People who begin to feel life threatened feel threatened first in terms of their societal roles: "Oh, will I be able to work?" "Will I be able to take care of my family?" "Can I take care of myself?" Later on they become threatened in terms of "Will I be extinguished?" The "I" that recognizes what I do or how I do things, knowing the world, what will happen to that? The fear that's associated with whether I don't exist takes place in those two realms, our postpersonal/societal, or our individual/personal existences.

Then there are three sequences in the life process that I call endings; middle ground; and new forming, or new beginnings. What I discovered in working with people is that most people see the process backwards. They see, "Oh, something new is beginning, I'm starting something new, something's on the horizon I'm excited about," and they focus a great deal on the futurizing aspects. What I think I found was that while all this organization for a tomorrow is going on, something is ending. The child could be seen as being born, which certainly it is, but it could also be seen as ending its uterine life. And it is very important how it ends its uterine life because that prepares the organization of birth—the signal to end being encapsulated—the way it begins to disengage itself from its container, the way it signals its good-bye to this life, is the essential ingredient of entering into the beginning of something else. The same is true for children. They end their childhood, and they begin to end it slightly before they begin to enter being an adolescent. You can watch the swinging back and forth between being an infant and struggling to be a child, ending by disorganizing the infant while the organization of the child is still being formed.

In ending something, which means taking down organization, taking down a structure, the investment in the body of our infancy has to be destructured in order for the organization of adulthood to manifest. But between disorganization and ending, and new form reorganizing, there is a middle ground, a place of transition, a place where there's clearly an ending to what was, and a very ill-defined what-will-be. And people oscillate among these three parts of their process: from what's ending, moderately without organizational form, and then beginning to move into practice of the new shape of existence. Disorganizations, endings, make a past; new organizations make a future; while middle ground is now. Time ends, and reforms, as do we. Dying is an ending of what is. And it has been going on in us since conception. We have ended our single-cell life, ended our two-celled life, and as we multiply in cellular complexity and organization, we keep ending the previous state of organizational life, always forming what can be called new form.

All endings bring with them grief and sadness for what was, a sense of loss, a dread of no future form, resentment at being cheated, relief from enduring, or shock and disbelief. People generally don't understand the full role of our emotional responses. Our emotional life is closer to the matrix of existence than our symbolic life, and the function of our feeling is to act as a bridge toward the next piece of behavior—it acts as the organizational substrata. In a simplified form, our emotional responses are connectors of our process, to what is and to what we hope will be. Our anger is a protest at what exists and, hopefully, it's a continuum of excitation toward a new behavior. Our sadnesses, our anxieties, our emotional tides stand between two structures as a bridge, between that which is ending and that which may form. Our emotional reactions are a part of our process of endings and in fact, the bridge which connects the person to others, to oneself, and to what will emerge. When our feelings are dismissed, cut off, disorganized, it is like a dying. When a connection of emotion is unformed, this too is a dying, an entering the void.

Our emotional life has a social communication, but it also has an intra-organismic or prepersonal and interpersonal meaning and communication. "I am angry," can mean "It's the only feeling that permits me a contact between how I want to be and how I am being." As we descend the ladder of civilized organization, that is, of language and of symbolic and ritualized actions, we find ourselves closer to the mainstream of life: the feeling of the process of existence that tells us about our personal, immediate state of aliveness and our link to the prepersonal, that great genetic and molecular anima of existence that is experienced by the self-reflective part of ourselves as a felt connection to the process that underlies all life. That is another way of saying that as our social and personal roles undergo the process of disorganization or ending, we stand a chance to touch something that is the substrata of those roles, to have a felt experience of the continuity of existence that comes from recognizing the continuity of unforming and reforming. That is the chance to know what is transcendent.

To be civilized is to have roles to perform: to be brave, to be self-sacrificing, to be wise, to be successful. So we have dying roles. The mythology of modern times is that death is simply a void, a nothingness; just as in religions, death is an entrance into a peopled heaven where we have social roles to perform. The good death during the Middle Ages was a public death. In the terminal stages of your dying, the door to your house was open, people came in and saw you, it was appropriate for you to forgive those people you felt had wronged you. It was very important that you face the East, to receive the Sacrament, to be open to the public, to share your life, and to forgive the wrongs against you. That is not the image of the good death now. The proper social role for a good death now is, "Shut up, don't complain, don't be a nuisance, go into hiding, and do it quietly and cheaply." Rilke, the poet, wrote about the death of his uncle. His uncle was given a special room where everyone was in contact. How he bellowed for attention, and service was given him. And all his foul tempers were part of the rite of dying—this was his chance to live everything that was unlived during his life. He was living his death—not the society's death, his death—ending his roles and forming his death.

We have a chance to live the program that nature has endowed us with. It's a choice that each and every one of us faces in trying to make emotional meaning of the story we are going to tell ourselves about the ending of our existence, or about what is waiting to greet us after this one. We have a choice as to what stories we wish to believe. Are we going to invest ourselves in the wisdom of the ancients, or are we going to permit ourselves to make our own story? All of us have the opportunity, in our little dyings—the changes and the transitions from one stage of life to another—to prepare for our dying, since endings are teachers.

Our personal death: How we wish to end, how we disembody, how we live our own process and die. We all have a psychological orientation toward our own endings. There are many people who want to secret themselves from most other people and die only in the intimacy of one-to-one, and not make their death a public, hospital one. There are many people who will tell you, "I do not want to die in an airplane crash—that is not my death; I do not want to die mutilated"; whereas another person will say to you, "An airplane crash is a good way to die; thirty seconds and you're finished." You will get from people, "I don't want to know it," as well as, "I want it to be slow and I want my friends around me, and I want to talk about it." You get from some people, "Quick," and from other people, "Slow." You get from some people, "I want to know," and from other people, "I don't want to know." And these become major orientations. In this way people tell us whether they want a private or a public dying, and in what way they want to organize themselves to end what was and is.

When you are accompanying people in their ending, there is a chance for them to live a hidden, prepersonal, or personal self. As they move from endings to middle ground they'll face the conflict: Should I go back, or move forward? And again, moving from middle ground to new beginnings, the same conflict. It is here I see the work: to support the shedding of images of who we should be; to allow who we are to emerge, as we assume the shape that indeed reflects the experience we live.

REFERENCES

Keleman, S. (1974). *Living your dying.* New York: Random House.
Keleman, S. (1979). *Somatic reality.* Berkeley: Center Press.

Death Is Forever—LIVING IS NOW

Abraham B. Brody

ABSTRACT. The author, in his 60s at the time this article was written, addresses his own fear of death and finally considers the consequences and limitations to life such a fear imposes. He offers a five-point guideline which grows out of his investigations as a psychotherapist and workshop leader.

I remember, during my adolescence, lying in bed, rigid and sweating, terrified at the thought of my inevitable death. Those panics occurred infrequently but persistently for a number of years. The eternity of nonexistence that lay before me, and my inability to alter it, overwhelmed me. I would lie awake until, with a great effort of will, I forced myself to think of other things and gradually relaxed enough to fall asleep.

As I grew into adulthood, the night terrors became less frequent and much less powerful. I had become more involved with life, and had also learned to repress my anxieties more effectively. Eventually, they no longer occurred.

During my analyses, I mentioned my fear of death, but never focused on it because of my conviction that nothing could be done about it and it was best left dormant. None of my analysts made significant efforts to explore these particular feelings with me. One of them responded with, ''If the eternity before you were born doesn't bother you, why should the eternity after you die?'' I felt then that his lack of sensitivity to the crucial issue (my present awareness of the temporary nature of my existence) simply confirmed my belief that my fears were so abnormal as to set me apart from other people.

When I reached my midsixties, I became aware that references to death, especially to the death of people my own age, made me feel uncomfortable, and were quickly put out of mind. Although the terror of my adolescence was not repeated, it became clear to me that I had repressed the fear and that as I grew older it was likely to become an increasingly serious problem. At this point, I came to a crucial realization: death itself was not the problem; being dead would not bother me. It was my fantasies

Abraham Brody, Ph.D., received his doctorate from Teachers College, Columbia University. He is engaged in the private practice of psychotherapy. Dr. Brody is on the faculty and Board of Advisors to Workshops of Living-Learning (WILL), Box 312, North Creek, NY 12853.

while alive and aware that troubled me. I had to be alive to be afraid of dying.

It had always been obvious to me that the inevitable end of my life was the source of my anxiety, but I had focused on my nonexistence as being the central issue. Now, I realized that the certainty of my ultimate death and my inability to affect it in any way was a very significant part of my fear. This awareness opened up new vistas for me. I know a good deal about my reaction to feelings of helplessness, and I know something about how to cope with them. Above all, "Don't just sit there! Do something!" Years of training as a psychologist had made it natural for me to react to such a demand by going to the library and doing some research.

Fortunately, the small but well-equipped local library had a bibliography (Miller & Acri, 1977) on death, published as a separate volume. An interesting sidelight is that while the book was in the reference department and not to be removed from the library, when I asked the librarian for special permission to take it out, she noticed the subject involved and said, "O. K. There isn't much chance anyone else will want to use it."

When I explored the literature, I was surprised to discover how many people had given a great deal of thought to the subject and written a tremendous amount about it. Further, I learned that many people, a number of whom I had read, respected, and learned from during my life, had also feared death; some even saw it as a universal human feeling. My fear of death was not a measure of my separateness from others, but one more evidence of my own humanness. I had only begun my exploration and these first steps had made a significant difference in my view of myself and my fears.

Early in my investigation I discovered Ernest Becker's *The Denial of Death* (1973), which I found both exciting and provocative. Starting with the ideas expressed by Becker, and incorporating the views of a number of other writers, I began to formulate my own version of the consequences of denying the fear of death, and the limitations this placed upon life and living.

First: Viewing life as a process, a series of changes and movements, makes it more difficult to avoid awareness of the end—the ultimate, inevitable death that lies ahead. One defense against this awareness is to deny, or at least to minimize, the notion of process; to seek stability—static, permanent, rigid stability; to avoid change, spontaneity, and creativity; to allow as few unknowns as possible to enter into living; to play it safe; to stick to the "tried and true" paths that have always been used; to not risk failures that will be reminders of human limitations.

Second: Reduce contact with, and awareness of, the processes of nature that are difficult, and, in some cases, impossible to influence; invest feelings in man-made things, in social and cultural goals; make money; become famous; get ahead of the other person. Even if you never achieve these goals, they are achievable, and some of us do manage it. Trying can at least keep one so busy that there is no time to think of the one thing no one can manage to achieve.

Third: Attain as much distance as possible from the concrete realities of physical existence. Attending to my body and the physical processes that must continue if I am to live brings a clearer awareness of the vulnerability of my biological structure. It takes so little to change the warm, living flesh and blood of my body into a pile of meat that must decay. Even while alive, a slow but inexorable decay takes place. Every day I die a little. So diets, exercises, cosmetics, and so forth are used, not to celebrate living, but to deny, or at least delay awareness of dying.

Fourth: Focus as much as possible on mental processes. In my own mind, anything is possible. I can dream of immortality and fantasize enough soap operas to keep my mind occupied and less aware of how weak and vulnerable I am, how small and meaningless compared with the enormity of the universe and of eternity.

Fifth: Identify with someone or something larger, more potent, and, hopefully, more durable than myself. Analysts help a little, as do teachers, athletes, presidents, heroes, and so forth. Institutions help even more, especially emotionally powerful ones like countries and religions. Finally, there is surely a noble and worthy object with which to identify— humanity itself. Trouble arises, of course, because this process of identification has a flip side of increasing my own feelings of insignificance, which makes further identification necessary and leads to a never-ending need for more and more identification with outside power and less and less reliance on my own power.

As my investigations continued, I experienced a release of energy that enabled me to develop my ideas in two directions: I began to organize a theoretical view in terms of the self system, that is, an organization of personality designed to avoid the anxiety aroused by the prospect of dying. And, I began to develop a workshop predicated on Theme-Centered Interactional principles (Cohn, 1969-70) which consisted of a series of themes designed to encourage people to face the reality of death and the anxiety it engendered; to then become aware of the defenses used to avoid this anxiety and how these defenses interfere with developing a full life. I entitled the workshop, "Death Is Forever—Living is Now."

I have given several of these workshops and it has been rewarding to help the participants begin to reduce their anxiety and increase their involvement in living more fully. Of course, a single workshop can only begin to modify the feelings and attitudes involved. Although many participants have come anticipating a grim experience, they have found, despite anxious moments, that they were able to face issues of living with more energy and effectiveness by the end of the workshop.

I myself, have experienced a similar increase in effectiveness, though the process is far from a smooth one. I have had periods of blocking and of anxiety which have been discouraging and frustrating, but never before have I organized my ideas on any subject into an article for publication nor felt as eager to continue my work as I do now.

I cannot alter the fact of my ultimate death, but I am able to affect my present feelings about dying and no longer feel helpless to cope with them.

REFERENCES

Becker, E. (1973). *The denial of death.* New York Free Press.
Cohn, Ruth C. (1969-1970). The theme-centered interactional method—Group therapists as group educators. *The Journal of Group Psychoanalysis and Process,* 2(2), 19-36.
Miller, A. J. & Acri, M. J. (1977). *Death: A bibliographical guide.* Metuchen, NJ & London: Scarecrow.